ISSUE 8

SUMMER 2014

WWW.THEPOINTMAG.COM

TABLE *of* CONTENTS

symposium: what is science for?

reviews

The Point is based in Chicago and published twice a year. Subscribe at *www.thepointmag.com* or correspond with us at info@thepointmag.com. *The Point* is grateful for the support of the Helen Zell Foundation, the Orphiflamme Foundation, Sheldon Baskin, and all of you who contributed to our successful Kickstarter campaign last year. Thank you!

LETTER FROM THE EDITORS:

THE NEW HUMANITIES

IN AUGUST OF last year the psychologist Steven Pinker took to the pages of the *New Republic* to defend the relevance of science to "humanistic scholarship." Science, he wrote, is "of a piece with philosophy, reason, and Enlightenment humanism," and should accordingly be recognized as contributing to investigations concerning "the deepest questions about who we are, where we came from, and how we define the meaning and purpose of our lives." A month later, the *New Republic*'s literary editor, Leon Wieseltier, fought back. The humanities are "the study of the many expressions of human inwardness," he argued, and therefore categorically inappropriate for the brand of empirical research advocated by Pinker. But Pinker, like the rest of the "scientizers," would not be satisfied with "consilience" between science and the humanities anyway; what he really wants, according to Wieseltier, is for "the humanities to submit to the sciences, and be subsumed by them."

The debate might as well have taken place in the 1960s, or in outer space. Pinker, the author of a recent doorstop on the virtues of a world created by scientific progress, behaves as if we were still living in the Dark Ages, alleging a "demonization campaign" against science led by powerful humanists such as the historian Jackson Lears and the ethicist Leon Kass (all Pinker has on his side are the administrations of nearly every research university in the country, not to mention the president of the United States). Wieseltier, on the other hand, trots out Tolstoy and Proust as if these nineteenth-century luminaries have anything to do with what is going on in contemporary English departments and philosophy workshops.

Ostensibly, Pinker and Wieseltier both address a question of disciplinary boundaries that arises within the modern research university, where the humanities denote a loose cluster of academic disciplines (Philosophy, English, Comparative Literature, Cultural Studies) devoted, supposedly, to the investigation of human arts and culture. But neither Tolstoy nor Proust were employed in the "humanities" in this sense (though it is fun to imagine Tolstoy's face during a typical meeting of the Slavic Languages faculty at Brown) and increasingly they are not even studied in them. Stanley Fish, Gerald Graff and Martha Nussbaum are employed in these academic humanities, and these days they spend much of their time writing books and articles attempting to justify what they do. This is because they know the "humanities scholar" to be a gravely endangered species.

Fish, Nussbaum and Graff do not agree about *why* the academic humanities are dying, or on what makes the best case for their survival. Their lack of consensus (Nussbaum believes the humanities make for better citizens, Graff that they offer benefits for the economy) makes the humanities appear vulnerable to the recommendations of an outsider like Pinker. Pointing to the declining number of students enrolling in the humanities (a 2011 report showed that, nationally, the percentage of humanities majors hovers around 7 percent—half what it was in 1970), as well as the increasing funding gap between them and the sciences, Pinker alleges that the problem with the humanities is that they have "failed to define a progressive agenda" like the sciences. Not only does this oversight perplex Pinker, it is positively incomprehensible to the "university presidents and provosts" he drinks Chardonnay with, many of whom

> have lamented to me that when a scientist comes into their office, it's to announce some exciting new research opportunity and demand the resources to pursue it. When a humanities scholar drops by, it's to plead for respect for the way things have always been done.

To which we say: "Ha!" And: "If only!"

Sadly, the respect of present-day humanities scholars for "the way things have always been done" ranks just barely above their respect for the presidency of George W. Bush. There might have been a time when the humanities offered a counterweight within the university to the sciences' relentless optimism and obsession with "progress," but since at least the 1970s—perhaps not incidentally when the enrollment numbers began to decline—only the heretics have stood up for anything resembling tradition. Today's humanities professors speak of nothing *but* "new research opportunities," nothing but "progress," nothing but the gross injustice of the "way things have always been done."

Wieseltier and Pinker's debate is thus academic in the pejorative sense. Wieseltier accuses Pinker of wanting the humanities to submit to the sciences; Pinker maintains that he simply wants the humanities to admit the relevance of scientific methods. Yet with a couple of exceptions (the Core at Columbia and the University of Chicago, the St. John's colleges, that place out in the California desert where they herd cattle while debating Plato) the scholarly humanities have admitted much more than the relevance of the sciences: they *have* submitted; they *have* been subsumed. "Imagine," writes Wieseltier,

> a scientific explanation of a painting—a breakdown of Chardin's cherries into the pigments that comprise them, and the chemical analysis of how their admixtures produce the subtle and plangent tonalities for which they are celebrated.

Wieseltier is right that such an explanation would tell us everything except what we most want to know about the painting, but he is mistaken if he thinks we need *imagine* such procedures.

In recent years, nothing has so captivated humanities scholars as the idea that brain science, evolutionary biology and the "new psychology" will lead to breakthroughs (not to mention funding) for their fields. Since 2000, Harvard's Elaine Scarry has hosted a seminar on cognitive theory and the arts, turning Harvard's Humanities Center into a colloquium for supposedly path-breaking lectures such as "Where Time and Memory Collide: *Maus* and the Neuroscience of Comics" and "Speech, Gesture, Bodily Stance: Studying Multimodal Communication in a Massive Data Set." Just two months before Pinker's article appeared, the *Nation* reported optimistically on students at Stanford being hooked up to functional magnetic resonance imaging (fMRI) so that their brain waves could be charted as they read *Mansfield Park*; on the same campus, English graduates are encouraged to gather in a "literature lab" where the only required language is computer code ("In this class there will be 1,200 books assigned," boasts one course description, "but students won't read any of them"). Not to be outdone, Duke has staked its claim to leadership with a "neurohumanities" major and study-abroad curriculum whose description ("a six-week, two-course program that brings a vertically integrated and international learning community into sustained dialogue to advance theorizations at the crossroads of neuroscience and humanities systems of knowledge and disciplinary milieu") we can only assume was written by artificial intelligence, while the *New York Times* reports, breathlessly, that the most advanced English professors are now "convinced science not only offers unexpected insights into individual texts, but that it may help to answer fundamental questions about literature's very existence." So it is not necessary to speculate theoretically on the role the sciences can play in the humanities; we can simply look, scientifically as it were, at the results so far.

Literary studies makes a good test case precisely because it is the field in which science has received the most extravagant embrace. A naïve onlooker might have been forgiven for assuming that this year's "Impression and Object" conference—home to such lectures as "From Thermodynamics to Critical Theory: The Politics of Émile Zola's Entropic Aesthetics" and "Digital Theophany: Affect and Software in the Cartographies Schizoanalytiques"—was being hosted by speculative chemists, as opposed to the CUNY Comparative Literature department. The concluding keynote address, delivered by Stanford professor Joshua Landy, continued the theme by examining the newest episode in the long and passionate courtship between literary studies and science, dubbed the "the cognitive turn." A lucid and clear writer, Landy has previously been the author of well-regarded literary scholarship on such topics as philosophical self-knowledge in Proust and the concept of "re-enchantment" in Mallarmé. There was reason to hope, therefore, that he would shed some genuine light—whether critical or favorable—on the latest trend to grip his discipline.

Landy began by cautioning for a few minutes about the dangers of excessive "scientism" or "neuromania"; literary scholars could be excitable, he allowed, and it was important not to assume that science was capable of solving all their problems. That said, the rest of Landy's talk was devoted to heralding the "extremely important work" currently being done at the intersection of literature and empirical psychology. What kind of work is this? Landy said he mostly valued empirical psychology for its ability to "verify" some of the claims that literary scholars have made in the past (for instance, "neurologists of reading" have shown that sound patterns *do* matter in poetry) and to disprove or "moderate" others (for example that reading Dickens makes us more empathetic, or that "all thoughts are linguistic"). Some literary theorists, he alleged, have argued that Virginia Woolf is not intrinsically superior to Dan Brown, and therefore that preferring Woolf is just snobbery. Fortunately the work of David Kidd and others shows there is a "measurable difference in outcome" between reading the two authors, meaning that evaluation doesn't merely come down to "invidious class distinctions or the desire to accrue capital."

No doubt we are thankful to science for "proving" that it is a different experience to read *To the Lighthouse* than it is to read *The Da Vinci Code*. But surely the cognitive turn must offer something more than this. Perhaps more promising is the study trumpeted on the front page of Duke's Neurohumanities website, which purports to offer a deeply original analysis of "data" collected from nineteenth-century British literature specialists for a study on "personality psychology." Here was the report's concluding statement:

> Overall, [the researchers] found that Victorian authors' depictions of personality and its impact on outcomes largely mirrored those established by modern psychology (e.g. female characters place more emphasis on extrinsic attributes in their love interests, while male more on physical attractiveness).

> They state that this realistic correspondence and recognizable psychology are necessary for readers to be able to understand the characters. ... Thus, by applying techniques developed in personality psychology to literature in an entirely original fashion, these authors were able to unearth an adaptive function in Victorian literature—opening the door for an entirely new domain of neurohumanities.

Beneath the jargon—it's as if the authors have turned the language of science against the standards of precision it was developed to satisfy—what exactly is going on here? This working group appears to have determined that Victorian novels are in part appreciated by readers because their characters have a similar psychology (well, a "realistic correspondence") to that of human beings. Does research like this meet the requirements of the progressive agenda Pinker is calling for? It certainly *says* it does. Notice how the vocabulary grows even more opaque as the report attempts to articulate its own value. What does it mean to "unearth an adaptive function in Victorian literature"? And what exactly is the "new domain" of research that has been discovered? For all its scientific ambition, the conclusion testifies to the neurohumanities community's inability to be objective about itself. It takes results that ought to encourage skepticism about the value of the neurohumanities and instead twists them into an endorsement for their significance.

But what does it mean, anyway, for something to be of significance in literary studies? The most striking thing about Landy's lecture, for us, was the question he never asked. How can Landy or anyone else assess what constitutes "extremely important work" in literary studies without considering what is important about literary studies as it stands? And to consider this demands asking what literary studies are *for*. If this question is left unasked, it must be for one of two reasons: either there is broad consensus as to the purpose of literary studies (as there is, say, with medicine), in which case the question would be superfluous; or there is no consensus whatsoever, in which case it would be futile. Anyone who has even a glancing acquaintance with modern-day literary studies departments (and Landy has more than that) knows the situation is the latter. Yet the absence of consensus about the purpose of literary studies may be less revealing than the lack of a sense, among literary studies professors, that one is needed.

Wieseltier's conviction that the humanities carry on the study of "human inwardness" is therefore not borne out in today's literary studies departments, where not only have scientific methods been welcomed with open arms, but there seems to be little confidence that humanistic scholarship has any unifying program that could distinguish it from the sciences *at all*.

WHAT WE CURRENTLY call the humanities should (mostly) be called the human sciences. What Landy is interested in has a name: it is called psychology. The professors who have recently struck Shakespeare and Chaucer from the required curriculum at UCLA, in favor of a mélange of gender, race and disability studies, are interested in (multi-)cultural history and political science. For decades, professors in English and Comparative Literature departments have been interested in linguistics, anthropology, sociology; at one time they were interested in psychoanalysis; further back than that, they did philology. All of these activities may have something to offer a robust literary studies but, notwithstanding the cheerleaders of consilience, at every "intersection" between fields a scholar must make the choice as to which discipline will lead the way. Literary studies may employ cognitive psychology in its attempt to better understand literary texts, but if it is driven by a psychological question (say, what is the effect of reading on moral sympathy?), then what is being done is psychology, not literary studies (and probably *bad* psychology, since it is carried out by people trained to read novels, not data sets).

But perhaps there is no longer any such thing as literary studies. It is not easy, after all, to find literature professors, at least in their roles as academics, who seem satisfied by what outsiders might naïvely assume to be the core function of something called literary studies: studying literature. Of course, this phrase is not as transparent as it might seem: What does it mean to study (as opposed to simply read) literature, and why would one be paid to do it? A more pointed way of asking the question is this: What do we, as readers, have to gain from someone who studies literature for a living?

There are many ways of answering that question: here is ours. We look to the literary scholar to tell us what is in, and at stake in, a work of literature. As someone who is presumed to have spent a long time with it, and therefore to have achieved an insight, born from experience, into its inner workings, the literary scholar is midwife to the literary work. "You speak from inside the poem as someone looking to see how the roof articulates with the walls and how the wall articulates with the floor," says Helen Vendler about the activity of criticism. "And where are the crossbeams that hold it up, and where are the windows that let light through?"

Reading Vendler on Emily Dickinson, or Stanley Cavell on Beckett, or James Wood on Norman Rush, or Zadie Smith on David Foster Wallace, enriches our sense of what is going on in the literature written by those authors, and of how their work addresses us as readers. Every work of art, said Hegel, enters into a conversation with everyone who encounters it. That conversation can be enriched by the literary critic, who has conversed with thousands of works of art (or a few, but very deeply). Ideally she enriches it to the point where it joins the larger conversation we are always having with ourselves, about ourselves—a conversation which encompasses the sciences without looking to them for validation, and whose subject both includes and exceeds the territory described by Wieseltier's "inwardness."

Yet it is difficult to contribute to such a conversation: there is no set methodology for it, and anyway most university professors deny it has anything to do with them. When we write our dissertations, we are told that we are doing "research," and this research is expected to be cumulative, objective. We therefore distance ourselves from those amateurs who continue to appeal to the humanities for reflection on such philistine topics as how to live or what to value. That is why the next turn, whether it be cognitive, or linguistic, or sabermetric, will no doubt be another turn *away* from the urgent questions that motivate most of us to pursue careers in the humanities in the first place.

This might seem a dire situation for the humanities; and it is, for the *academic* humanities. Fortunately, the humanities have always been bigger than the academic humanities. Unlike in the sciences, to participate in the conversation about what it means to be human does not require an advanced degree (increasingly it seems to be impeded by it)—which is why it should come as no surprise that the humanities are often more aggressively defended by magazine editors and op-ed columnists than by academics. In Wieseltier's case, the argument for the sanctity of the academic humanities eventually tilts over into a call for what he calls the "old humanities," examples of which (like Vendler's recent piece on Dickinson) abound in the brilliant Books section over which he has stood guard since 1983.

Around the turn of the century, it may have seemed that the humanities were more endangered outside of academia than within it, given that their institutional framework (paper-and-ink magazines) was giving way. Against the predictions of doom-by-technology, however, the intervening years have seen the emergence of a series of online and print publications (*n+1*, *LA Review of Books*, the *Believer*, the *New Inquiry*) devoted to political and cultural analysis and to the close examination of art, television and literature. Those who write for these magazines are not opposed to academia; many of them are academics themselves—and it is not hard to find examples of articles corrupted by that association. Yet in the best pages of these magazines and websites, authors meet their audiences not as researchers but as readers and critics, showing us where the windows are that let the light in.

The new humanistic writing and its enthusiastic readership bear witness to the fact that, as long as there are human beings, there will remain an interest in scholarship and criticism that attempts to illuminate human problems. As we wait (and we will wait forever) to taste the milk and honey promised by Pinker's "digital humanities," we can only hope that academics will muster the courage to glance up from their research and join that conversation. In the meantime, to those perplexed, or simply disappointed, by the state of the academy, we say: Read a magazine!—starting with this one.

essays

Kara Walker, *no world*, 2010
All images from *An Unpeopled Land in Uncharted Waters*
Courtesy of the artist and Sikkema Jenkins & Co., New York

*transcendence

THE PROBLEM OF SLAVERY

DAVID BRION DAVIS'S PHILOSOPHICAL HISTORY

by Scott Spillman

THE 2013 BEST PICTURE *12 Years a Slave* tells the story of Solomon Northup, a free black man living in New York who was kidnapped in 1841, sold in Louisiana, held for twelve years as a slave, and finally freed in 1853. The film succeeds for many reasons, not the least of which is its uncompromising take on the slave South. It also helps, I think, that Northup's story neatly encapsulates the whole history of New World slavery: the initial capture and sale, the anger and despair of losing freedom and family, the dehumanizing effects of slave society, the accommodations and adjustments necessary for survival, and the return to a problematic freedom. We see it all unfold through one man's eyes—his pain, his compromises and, finally, his relief upon returning home to his family.

It's important that Northup (Chiwetel Ejiofor) starts and ends the movie as a free man. Logically, this shouldn't make much of a difference in how we perceive the horrors of slavery. If slavery is truly evil, it shouldn't matter whether a person is born into slavery or enslaved later in life; in either case, a free and equal human being has been reduced to a piece of property, like an ox. This is precisely why the sight of a free black man living happily with his family served as the strongest possible rebuke to any racial justification of slavery. In the film, the early scenes of Northup working and taking care of his family in the North exacerbate the viewer's sense of the injustice and brutality of what follows. Though compelled to work as a slave, Northup never becomes a slave to his desires, challenging by his restraint and silence the dehumanizing gaze of his successive masters.

As *12 Years a Slave* repeatedly shows, the idea that black slaves were something less than human—although appealing for obvious reasons to masters—was subject to an inevitable tension, first at the abstract level of argument and then, more fatally, at the concrete level of daily life. The movie's signal achievement is to bring out the various consequences of this tension, perhaps most powerfully in the relationship between the white master Edwin Epps (Michael Fassbender) and his slave girl Patsey (Lupita Nyong'o). Epps, who repeatedly refers to his slaves as his "property" and compares them to baboons, nevertheless warns his jealous wife that he would sooner send her away than lose Patsey. Later, in one of the film's most memorable scenes, Epps is himself driven into a jealous rage by his suspicion that Patsey has escaped his control and cheated on him with a neighbor. Unable to whip Patsey himself, he compels Northup to do it. As Northup draws blood, Epps looks on with a blend of satisfaction, hatred and horror utterly belying his claim that Patsey means no more to him than a ball of yarn or a beast of prey.

For the historian David Brion Davis, this dynamic describes the basic "problem" of slavery. Ideally, as Aristotle noted long ago, a slave is like a tool or a domestic animal—something the master owns and over which he has complete control. Yet such a "natural slave" has never existed; and no system of slavery has ever successfully dehumanized its slaves to the point where they are indistinguishable from mere property. This inherent contradiction led, according to Davis, not only to complicated relationships between masters and their slaves, but to organized opposition, for which "the essential issue was how to recognize and establish the full and complete humanity of a 'dehumanized people.'"

When and how the contradiction of treating a person as property became enough of a moral issue that people would demand an end to slavery is the question that has occupied the bulk of Davis's career, especially in the three long works culminating with *The Problem of Slavery in the Age of Emancipation*, which he completed this year at the age of 86. Reviewing that final volume for the *Nation*, the historian Eric Foner described the Problem of Slavery trilogy as one of the "towering achievements of historical scholarship of the past half-century," while in the *New York Review of Books* Drew Gilpin Faust credited Davis's practice of "embedding ideas in social and political action" with "shap[ing] scholars and scholarship for decades to come."

It is possible that even this high praise undervalues the scope and power of Davis's contribution. Although the latest volume is belated and in many ways inferior to the previous two, it demonstrates, particularly in its focus on "dehumanization," what distinguishes Davis not just as a historian but as a thinker with relevance far beyond his field. Is slavery a sin? What exactly constitutes our "full and complete humanity"? Because he considers such questions not just historically but also philosophically, Davis's research opens out, like *12 Years a Slave*, into broader topics such as freedom, forgiveness, and the possibility of transcendence. Slavery, Davis saw, was a profoundly human problem, and therefore to reckon with slavery would mean to reckon with human nature—that is, to reckon with the kind of being that was simultaneously capable of perpetrating such a system and also of coming to see the need to dismantle it.

EMANCIPATION AND THE end of slavery didn't end the dehumanization of blacks in America, of course. After the brief interlude of Reconstruction, there followed decades of lynchings based upon the myth of the "black beast" rapist and nearly a century of Jim Crow segregation. In fact, Davis's emphasis on exploring dehumanization through concrete moral problems derives from his experiences growing up in the racially segregated America of the mid-twentieth century, especially his service in a segregated army in Germany right after the end of World War II.

Davis was born in Denver, in 1927, to parents of a writerly and artistic persuasion. His father, a journalist turned novelist turned screenwriter, took the family around the country as he switched newspapers and professions: Seattle, Buffalo, Carmel, Los Angeles, Manhattan. Traveling with them the whole time was Davis's grandmother who, born in 1861, remembered hearing the news of Lincoln's assassination on her family's front porch. When Davis graduated from high school more than eighty years later, in 1945, he had never shared a classroom with a black student. Such were the realities of race in America in the middle of the twentieth century.

Three days after graduation, Davis headed to basic training at Camp Gordon in Georgia to prepare for the invasion of Japan. This was his first time in the Deep South, and the depths of its racism shocked him. When Hiroshima and Nagasaki ended the war in Japan in August, the young recruits suddenly received a new mission for which they were not particularly well prepared: police work in postwar Germany. On the ship to Europe, an officer gave Davis a club and told him to go downstairs and "keep the 'jiggaboos' from gambling." The army was still segregated in those days, and the ship contained two thousand black soldiers in its lower holds, as Davis was surprised to discover when he descended the staircase. "I came upon what I imagined a slave ship would have looked like," he later recalled. "Hundreds and hundreds of near-naked blacks jammed together, many of them shooting craps." One of them glanced up at Davis. "What you doin' down here, white boy?" he asked. Davis hid in the shadows for four hours, until his shift was up.

Davis served as part of the army's security police in Mannheim and Stuttgart. His commander was obsessed with rumors of Nazi conspiracies and spent his days trying to root out supposed neo-Nazi meetings. For his part, Davis had

Kara Walker, *beacon (after R.G.)*, 2010

been horrified by the revelations that followed the liberations of Dachau and Bergen-Belsen that spring. On the ground in Mannheim, however, he found the Germans warm and friendly. Most were simply glad not to be in the Russian sector (which would later become East Germany). Davis made friends with young men who were interested in American culture and willing to help investigate the black market. Meanwhile, young German women proved eager to dance and drink beer with the soldiers. Davis recalled that there was no prostitution in Mannheim: "Americans joked that there was simply too much nonprofessional competition."

But the German women didn't care whether the soldiers they dated were white or black, and that caused trouble. White soldiers fumed about "the God-damned black sonsabitches" who dated German women; a major general was cheered for saying it had been a mistake to send black troops to Europe. One night Davis and the other security police were called out to a dance club where black and white American troops had been fighting over the issue; blood already covered the sidewalk and the dance floor. Davis's commander soon got into a shouting match with a black captain, who represented about a dozen unarmed black troops. "Our lieutenant ordered us to pull back the bolts of our submachine guns, so we were ready to fire into this crowd of blacks," Davis recalled. Just then a white major marched in and cut the tension by calling everyone to attention. Even some sixty years later, Davis remembered this incident as "probably the scariest event in my life."

Davis noted the contrast between the Germans, who were supposedly Aryan-supremacist Nazis yet welcomed Americans regardless of race, and the Americans, who had supposedly fought for freedom and democracy yet maintained a segregated army. "Perhaps I sound a bit shrill," he wrote home at the time, "but it is difficult not to become alarmed when not one or two but dozens of men openly proclaim their hatred of the black race and take every opportunity to shoot or arrest or beat up colored soldiers." Looking back, he concluded, "I strongly suspect that this experience in Germany influenced my later decision to devote over forty years to the study of slavery and race."

Davis had already decided to become a historian. The idea first occurred to him while he was on R&R in Nice a month after the close call in Mannheim. He explained his reasoning to his parents in a long letter that fall, just before he returned to America:

> When we think back into our childhood, it doesn't do much good to merely hit the high spots and remember what we want to remember—to know why we act the way we do, we have to remember everything. ... Perhaps such teaching could make us understand ourselves. It would show

> the present conflicts to be as silly as they are. And above all, it would make people stop and think before blindly following some bigoted group to make the world safe for Aryans or democrats or Mississippians.

Back in the United States, Davis enrolled at Dartmouth on the G.I. Bill. He wanted to study history, but the department was so weak that he turned to philosophy instead. Interested in the history of political thought, he took a lecture course taught by Francis Gramlich about changing views of human nature. The course, culminating with a reading of Reinhold Niebuhr's *The Nature and Destiny of Man*, introduced Davis to the ideas that would guide his career for more than half a century. From Niebuhr, Davis learned to think of the central human problem as arising from the tension between the reality of mortality and the desire for transcendence. This tension leads, according to Niebuhr, to sin. Some humans deny their capacity for transcendence and become immersed in the material world of sensuality. Others—one thinks here of totalitarian dictators—deny their limitations by cultivating a tremendous self-pride, usually paired with an equally tremendous contempt for other, lesser humans.

After graduating in 1950, Davis tried to find a job in journalism, failed, and then began graduate school at Harvard's History of American Civilization program. But as with Dartmouth's history department, Davis found Harvard's American Civilization program unsatisfying. The program was devoted in those days to tracing different "isms" in American thought: Rationalism, Neoclassicism, Romanticism, an endless stream of abstractions that flowed into and out of one another. That kind of detached intellectual history didn't interest Davis at all. "I was taken by the notion of studying *concrete* human problems," he explained years later, "as a way of tracing, within social and cultural frameworks, broad shifts in beliefs, moral values, assumptions, and ideology."

The desire to study intellectual history through human responses to lived experience led Davis, initially, to look at homicide. He wanted to write his dissertation as a large interdisciplinary study of homicide in American history, but he also needed to research and write the whole thing in a single year. Need won out and Davis focused on attitudes toward homicide in early nineteenth-century American fiction. "Homicide," he wrote, "despite its many changing social and legal implications, is a universal problem, the culmination of all human aggression, and an ever-present means for the resolution of conflict." In retrospect, one can see Davis beginning to apply the Niebuhrian framework to human social relations, something he would do far more explicitly in his treatment of human slavery—"the archetype," he later wrote, "of this [Niebuhrian] sin of pride and contempt for others."

IN THE SPRING of 1955, while Davis was still in Cambridge trying to finish his dissertation, he met Kenneth Stampp. Stampp taught at Berkeley, but he was spending the semester as a visiting professor at Harvard. At the time, Stampp had nearly completed a book about American slavery—the first history of American slavery in a generation, since well before World War II. As Stampp talked to him about slavery and race, Davis realized that he had learned little about the subjects during his years at Dartmouth and Harvard. He later recalled "the awkwardness and embarrassment surrounding the study of slavery in the early 1950s."

The academic study of American history as we know it today emerged in the late nineteenth century at places like Cornell, Johns Hopkins, Columbia and Harvard. The idea was to make the study of history objective by focusing on the evolution of laws and institutions, much as a biologist might trace the evolution of a species. The studies of slavery that came out of these schools were narrow investigations, often focused on individual states, which actively avoided saying anything controversial or even noteworthy. The only real attempt to grapple with American slavery as a whole came from James Ford Rhodes, a Northern industrialist who had retired and moved to Cambridge to write his multivolume *History of the United States from the Compromise of 1850*. Rhodes focused mostly on politics, but in his first volume, published in 1892, he paused between the presidencies of Millard Fillmore and Franklin Pierce for a comprehensive eighty-page chapter called "Slavery." "It is my wish to describe the institution as it may have appeared before the war to a fair-minded man," he wrote. "Nevertheless, this chapter can only be a commentary on the sententious expression of Clay: 'Slavery is a curse to the master and a wrong to the slave.'"

Though Rhodes's history was greeted with great praise, it also provoked a reaction among Southerners who felt that their peculiar institution had been unfairly maligned. Already in the 1870s, as the North retreated from Reconstruction, Vice President Henry Wilson had recognized that the South, "though accepting the destruction of slavery, still believes it to be the proper condition of an inferior race, and the corner-stone of the most desirable civilization." By the 1890s Southerners admitted that slavery may have been evil, but they maintained it had served an important social purpose. "The time has gone by when it was necessary to exaggerate the evils of slavery in order to nurse the passions of men for its overthrow," one Tennessee-born historian wrote in a review of Rhodes's first two volumes. "The time has arrived for the cooler impartial study of the nature of this temporary relation between the highly civilized white race and the deeply barbarous negro race."

In 1893, the year after Rhodes's first volume was published, the historian Frederick Jackson Turner, speaking at a historical congress held at the World's

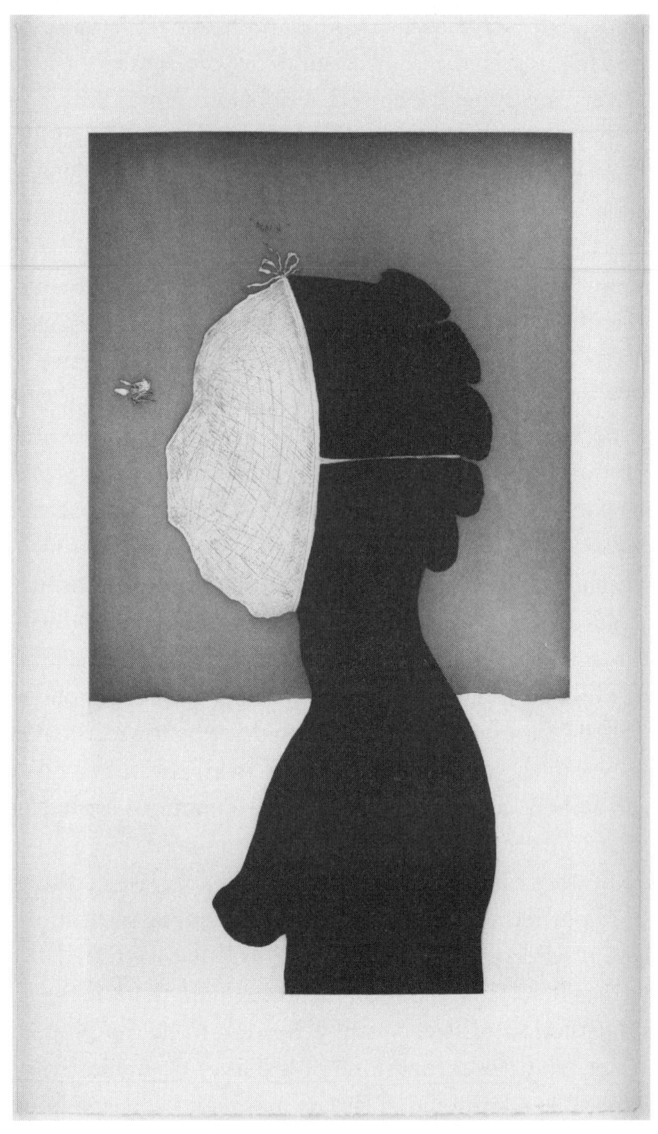

Kara Walker, *savant*, 2010

Fair in Chicago, urged Americans to forget their divisive slavery struggle and focus on their cooperative push west. Far more important than the "slavery question" was expansion along the western frontier, which had nurtured American individualism and democracy while also providing a field for the growth of national legislation and transportation. These economic, political and social developments were the real story of American history, Turner maintained. "Even the slavery struggle," he said, "occupies its important place in American history because of its relation to westward expansion."

The Progressive historians who followed Turner largely downplayed the importance of slavery, arguing that even the Civil War was primarily a struggle between the industry of the North and the agriculture of the South, as opposed to a battle over the future of slavery. One exception was Ulrich B. Phillips, who taught alongside Turner for half a decade at Wisconsin in the early twentieth century. Phillips was born in 1877, the year Reconstruction ended, in a part of Georgia that W. E. B. Du Bois once called "the center of the Negro problem,—the center of those nine million men who are America's dark heritage from slavery and the slave-trade." He made a career out of studying slavery and the slave plantation's role in driving American expansion across the old Southwest. This culminated in *American Negro Slavery*, which in 1918 became the first full history of slavery—as opposed to the political debates over slavery—in the United States.

Phillips finished *American Negro Slavery* while he was serving at Camp Gordon, Georgia, during World War I. This was the same camp where Davis would train a generation later for World War II. But in contrast to Davis, who was appalled by his first real experience with segregation, Phillips relished his return to the South after years of teaching at Michigan. The black soldiers training there seemed, to him, the same as plantation slaves of old. They "show the same easy-going, amiable, serio-comic obedience and the same personal attachments to white men, as well as the same sturdy light-heartedness and the same love of laughter and of rhythm, which distinguished their forbears," he noted. Phillips acknowledged that slavery might have had its share of horrors, but in general—good Progressive that he was—he saw it as a school or a settlement house in which benevolent whites could train barbarous blacks for civilization. "There were injustice, oppression, brutality and heartburning in the régime,—but where in the struggling world are these absent?" he concluded. "There were also gentleness, kind-hearted friendship and mutual loyalty to a degree hard for him to believe who regards the system with a theorist's eye and a partisan squint."

Despite its assumption of black inferiority, Phillips's work continued to dominate the study of American slavery well into the civil rights period. Davis's new friend Kenneth Stampp hoped to change that. Essentially, Stampp applied the lessons of the burgeoning civil rights movement to reverse Phillips's racist assumptions. "Innately Negroes *are*, after all, only white men with black skins, nothing more, nothing less," he wrote. He was willing, as Phillips was not, to treat black people as human beings, which meant considering "what slavery meant to the Negro and how he reacted to it." In *The Peculiar Institution*, published in 1956—just two years after *Brown v. Board*—he took Phillips's framework and evidence, substituted an antislavery perspective and a sympathy for the slaves, and produced a point-by-point rebuttal. The combination of Stampp's work and the civil rights movement irrevocably changed the way historians wrote about American slavery, making it impossible to look at slavery without considering the experiences of the slaves themselves. But it remained unclear whether anyone had learned anything fundamentally new about slavery. Stampp's basic points were, after all, a return to what the abolitionists had said a century earlier; he was still involved in an old debate about whether slavery was good or evil, and whether blacks were inferior or equal.

One historian who tried to get outside the increasingly tired moral and economic debate that had occupied historians like Rhodes, Phillips and Stampp for decades was Stanley Elkins. Elkins was less interested in arguing about whether slavery was good or bad, profitable or ruinous, than he was in figuring out how to study its effects on human behavior. In *Slavery*, published in 1959, he attempted to use the lessons of World War II to investigate the psychological consequences of slavery. In particular, he hypothesized that information about prisoners in German concentration camps might provide some insight into how oppressive institutions affected the psychology of their victims. He thought there might be some basis in reality for "Sambo," the childlike stereotype of the black slave who was "docile but irresponsible, loyal but lazy, humble but chronically given to lying and stealing." "The only mass experience that Western people have had within recorded history comparable in any way with Negro slavery was undergone in the nether world of Nazism," he explained, recounting how the camps destroyed the personality of prisoners and reduced them to children who identified with their masters. This was a role that survivors were taught to play. "If the concentration camp could produce in two or three years the results that it did," Elkins suggested, "one wonders how much more pervasive must have been those attitudes, expectations, and values which had, certainly, their benevolent side and which were accepted and transmitted over generations."

ELKINS'S WORK PROVOKED a generation of scholars who set out to show that slaves, far from becoming childlike drones, had developed a complex culture of their own. Davis's early writing on slavery reflected Elkins's influence in a different way. Davis was interested in slavery's psychological consequences—for its victims as well as its perpetrators—but primarily as the gateway to what he called a "problem of moral perception." Given that the inherent contradictions of treating a person as a "conveyable possession" had been a "source of latent tension" for centuries, the true intellectual riddle was how it had suddenly come to be seen as an intolerable evil. "The central question, the absolutely central question that fascinated me," he wrote, "was, given the fact that slavery evoked virtually no moral protest in a wide range of societies and cultures for literally thousands of years, how could we explain the emergence of a new moral perception by the mid-to-late eighteenth century?" This was the question that drove the narrative of *The Problem of Slavery in Western Culture*, Davis's 500-page "introductory volume" to his projected history of antislavery movements.

New World slavery in the eighteenth century was not uniquely evil; men in the eighteenth century were not uniquely virtuous. Slavery had existed in the West for thousands of years, and it had the considerable weight of classical philosophy and Christian accommodationism, as well as centuries of experience, behind it. It simply seemed like a necessary part of human society, a consequence of our sinful nature as humans. But it also seemed like a clear source of conflict, fear and philosophical contradiction. "The underlying contradiction of slavery became more manifest," Davis noted, "when the institution was closely linked with American colonization, which was also seen as affording mankind the opportunity to create a more perfect society." At roughly the same time, a complex series of developments in Western intellectual culture was changing the way many people thought about human nature, equality and individual freedom. Some Enlightenment thinkers relied on natural laws to sweep away traditional authorities, while others emphasized the basic inner goodness of human beings and recommended a new ethic of benevolence. The rise of evangelical religion reinforced both the burden on humans to do good in the world and the belief that all were capable of spiritual redemption. Africans began to be seen as not only barbarous and beastly, but also innocent and potentially virtuous. "By the eve of the American Revolution," Davis concluded, "there was a remarkable convergence of cultural and intellectual developments which at once undercut traditional rationalizations for slavery and offered new modes of sensibility for identifying with its victims."

Reviewing *The Problem of Slavery in Western Culture* in the *New York Review of Books*, the ancient historian Moses Finley concluded that Davis's book was

Kara Walker, *the secret sharerer,* 2010

"one of the most important to have been published on the subject of slavery in modern times." Yet Finley also found the book frustrating on the "decisive question" of *why* slavery was finally abolished in the West. Davis had written a successful history of ideas, explaining how it became possible for large groups of people to believe that slavery was a moral wrong. But even after this shift in moral perception enabled abolitionist thought to emerge, antislavery ideas did not triumph overnight. The intellectual possibility of abolitionism did not translate directly into government policy. New World slavery was still alive and well at the end of the book. "Nothing is more difficult perhaps than to explain how and why, or why not, a new moral perception becomes effective in action," Finley wrote. "Yet nothing is more urgent if an academic historical exercise is to become a significant investigation of human behavior with direct relevance to the world we now live in." He added, hopefully, "it may be that what I am looking for will find its proper place in the next volumes."

Davis did wrestle with these questions in his next volume, *The Problem of Slavery in the Age of Revolution* (1975). The book actually dealt with two problems. The first problem was the same as before, the moral and philosophical contradictions that come from insisting on treating a person as a thing. The second problem was the new problem, described by Finley, of how exactly abstract ideas fed into social movements, which then led to political change. Davis worked to trace these dynamics over the course of a fifty-year period that saw political revolutions in America, France and Haiti, as well as an economic revolution that gave rise to industrial production and mass wage labor.

Much of the thinking and writing took place at the Center for Advanced Study in the Behavioral Sciences at Stanford, where Davis received a yearlong fellowship in 1972. (By this time Davis had also moved from Cornell to Yale.) He happened to share his year there with Eugene Genovese, who was hard at work on his own big book about slavery, eventually published in 1974 as *Roll, Jordan, Roll: The World the Slaves Made*. Genovese's interpretation of Southern slavery placed a strong emphasis on paternalism, an ideology that supposedly helped mediate the contradictions inherent in slavery by covering them in a web of human relationships, with masters serving as protectors and providers to their childlike slaves. During their year in California, he and Davis worked together in what Davis called "an informal seminar on the general themes of dominance and submission." They exchanged drafts and had long talks, and the influence of each on the other's work is clear. Genovese's Marxist perspective on capitalism and labor loomed large in the background of Davis's *Age of Revolution*.

Yet Davis was too subtle of a thinker to apply the Marxist lens without augmentation. Indeed, the historian George M. Fredrickson praised Davis's second volume precisely for reviving a form of intellectual history respectful of the link between, "on the one hand, social and economic realities and, on the other, the realm of abstract ideas and principles." When Davis wrote about "ideology," for instance, he did not mean it simply as a rationalization for economic interests, but saw it rather as an evolving set of principles or values, *influenced* by economic conditions but certainly not reducible to them.

This distinction was important especially because the core of Davis's argument in *Age of Revolution* involved the functions of the antislavery movement in the emerging republican and capitalist ideologies of the late eighteenth and early nineteenth centuries. The ideology of antislavery, he wrote, "must be understood as part of a larger transformation in attitudes toward labor, property, and individual responsibility." This transformation resulted in a shift in perceptions of dominance and degradation. Slavery became a problem that was used to test the outer limits of new societal attitudes and political arrangements: What was freedom? What was labor? Were the citizens properly virtuous?

In the United States, one of the functions of antislavery ideas was to allow Americans to show that they were virtuous republicans whose revolution had not been about their own self-interest. More generally, abolitionism posited a hard distinction between slavery and other forms of labor. Entrepreneurial Quakers and others like them needed an outlet for the expression of Christian humanitarian ideals that would not also undercut their own business; the antislavery movement provided that, giving a "certain moral insulation to economic activities less visibly dependent on human suffering and injustice." This was not only a question of "economic interest," according to Davis, but also one of ideological function. Antislavery ideology supplied a simplified definition of freedom as the freedom to receive wages for one's labor. Monetary compensation, not physical coercion, became the acceptable means of labor discipline. Though this view of freedom was narrow, it was uncomplicated and made sense to the men who were developing the new economic order of industrial capitalism. "They unwittingly drew distinctions and boundaries which opened the way," Davis wrote, "under a guise of moral rectitude, for unprecedented forms of oppression."

As a result of the eighteenth-century shift in moral perception regarding slavery as well as the new thoughts and experiences that emerged from the American, French, Haitian and Industrial revolutions, the Age of Revolution served as "a major turning point in the history of New World slavery." The disruptiveness of war and the ideals of revolutionaries meant that slavery had been disavowed in principle and in practice in much of the West. Blacks as well as whites had gained a new consciousness of their own rights; and in England especially, a line had been drawn: slavery was bad, wage labor was good. But the revolutions that gave birth to these changes also increased the relative political power of the few remaining slaveholding regions, such as the American South and Brazil, whose defenses of slavery hardened in reaction to revolutionary-era antislavery agitation. By the 1820s, the two sides of the slavery question were headed down separate paths—paths that would, in the case of the United States, rip the country apart.

THE PROBLEM OF *Slavery in Western Culture* was published in 1966. It won the Pulitzer Prize. *The Problem of Slavery in the Age of Revolution* was published in 1975. It won the National Book Award. Davis planned a third volume to cover a nearly seventy-year period beginning with the push for abolition in Britain, and ending when Brazil became the final country in the New World to abolish slavery. "From the very start," he has noted, "I realized that this final volume of the project, on the 'Age of Emancipation,' would present the most formidable problems of coverage, selectivity, organization, and method." The slave emancipations of the nineteenth century involved, after all, an international movement whose success was bound up with the social, economic and cultural changes that we think of as making the modern world. To write a book about this process in the same capacious style Davis used in the earlier volumes would seem to require decades of research and thousands of pages.

It took him almost forty years but Davis finally completed *The Problem of Slavery in the Age of Emancipation* earlier this year.* Although the book does not satisfy all of the expectations raised by his earlier volumes, it nevertheless offers us insight into the fundamental ideas that have animated his work from the beginning. The first volume in the trilogy explored how it became possible for a large number of people "to perceive—in a moral sense—the inherent contradictions" of a system of slavery based on the principle that a person could be property. The second volume examined how the antislavery movement emerged in a world that was being transformed by the rise of republicanism and industrial

* Not that Davis was idle during this period. In 1986 he published "an exploratory pilot study," *Slavery and Human Progress*, which examined what Davis called the "momentous shift" from an older view of slavery as an agent of social and economic progress to a newer idea that modern, progressive societies were defined in large part by the absence of slavery. Following that, he published several collections of old articles and reviews, anthologies of historical documents and short books based on lectures, including the excellent but often overlooked *Revolutions: Reflections on American Equality and Foreign Liberations* (1990). He also became involved in an effort to improve history education in America, primarily through a series of summer seminars for high school teachers, and worked with the philanthropists Richard Gilder and Lewis Lehrman to establish the Gilder Lehrman Center for the Study of Slavery, Resistance, and Abolition at Yale in 1998.

Kara Walker, *buoy*, 2010

capitalism. The final volume hovers over the period from the 1790s to the 1860s; it is a "highly selective study" covering the Haitian Revolution, African colonization, black abolitionists and British and American emancipation. Because of this, it feels more like a collection of essays than its two prequels; however, the chapters are tied together by a common theme.

Although the concept of dehumanization—of treating people as animals or things—had been crucial to the arguments in the first two books of the trilogy, Davis rarely used the term or explored its meaning in detail. In *Age of Emancipation*, however, he focuses squarely on "dehumanization and its implications—the treatment of slaves as if they were domesticated animals and the continuing need of African Americans to confront and counteract the kind of white psychological exploitation that deprived them of the respect and dignity needed for acceptance as equals in a white society." It is this focus on dehumanization that leads Davis to place attitudes about free blacks at the center of his study of slave emancipation. He repeats several times a quote by Frederick Douglass, himself a free black man who had escaped slavery. "The most telling, the most killing refutation of slavery," Douglass told Harriet Beecher Stowe, "is the presentation of an industrious, enterprising, thrifty and intelligent free black population."

Yet many whites considered the prospect of free blacks living alongside them as perhaps the strongest argument *against* emancipation. In fact it was this prospect that made abolition in America much more difficult than in Britain, where slavery was confined to Caribbean islands with relatively few permanent white residents. Proposals for ending slavery in America always raised the question of what to do with the freed slaves. Simply to accept them as fellow citizens did not seem to be an option: some thought blacks really were racially inferior and incapable of governing themselves; others (including even some blacks) believed they had been so degraded by slavery and racial prejudice that they could never survive peacefully as free people in America. Either way, the effects of dehumanization pointed to the impossibility of incorporating blacks into free society.

Acts of abolition such as the Haitian Revolution of the 1790s and British emancipation in the 1830s always carried competing lessons regarding the capabilities of free blacks. As the first nationwide emancipation in the New World, Haiti loomed in the background of all later debates. It resulted in the world's first example of a free black republic made up of former slaves, an example that gave hope to free blacks and slaves around the Atlantic. But its violence also provided whites with plenty of evidence that blacks were too dangerous and dehumanized to be set free. The planter Bryan Edwards described the fate of one pregnant white woman: "The monsters, whose prisoner she was, having first murdered her husband in her presence, ripped her up alive, and threw the infant to the hogs.—They then (how shall I relate it) sewed up the head of her murdered husband in———!!!" This was a none-too-subtle lesson in what could happen if bestial blacks were not kept under tight control.

These and other perceived horrors influenced the development of the colonization movement, institutionalized in 1817 with the founding of the American Colonization Society, which attracted support from the likes of Henry Clay and Andrew Jackson. Although Davis doesn't endorse the colonizationist solution of deporting free blacks to Africa, he is sympathetic to the way its advocates wrestled with the problem of dehumanization, which abolitionists (not to mention many of the initial historians of slavery) tended to gloss over in a way that now seems naïve. "The simple dichotomy between the ACS Antichrist and the abolitionist Redeemers ... can only obscure our understanding of both movements," he writes, continuing:

> Although colonizationists have conventionally been dismissed as hopelessly impractical visionaries, for example, they were clearly more realistic than the abolitionists when they argued that white racial prejudice would remain intractable for generations to come, that the achievements of a few individual blacks would not benefit the masses, that progress would depend on black solidarity and collective effort, and that the formal act of emancipating slaves could not be divorced from the need for an economic and social environment in which freedmen could exercise their full capacities for human development.

Each of these points about the effects of black dehumanization was correct, and yet colonization was the wrong conclusion to draw from them. By emphasizing the problems facing blacks in America and the better lives they could make in some foreign land, colonizationists implied that blacks had been so dehumanized by slavery that they could not survive in an American society that was defined as white. This strategy, Davis writes, continued in new forms into the twentieth century and has proved "deceptive precisely because it is seldom cynical and has often been combined with genuine goodwill."

But blacks were not like a tumor, an alien growth in the American organism that could be easily isolated and removed. They formed a crucial strand of its DNA. "The glaring defect in the colonizationist ideology," Davis notes, "was the refusal to recognize the vital contributions that blacks had made and would continue to make to American civilization." Their reaction against the white colonization movement spurred free blacks to assert their own humanity and fitness for free society against the dehumanizing impulses of slavery and racism.

This proves to be the development on which *Age of Emancipation* hinges. Some free blacks supported colonization when the movement first started in the 1810s, but most had turned against it by the 1820s. Free blacks like Northup, who had built lives and families in the only country they had ever called home, argued that colonization was a ploy to strengthen slavery by removing only blacks who weren't slaves, thereby removing any reminders that they might be well suited for freedom. When a man like Northup could make a living from his talent as a musician, the theory that blacks formed an inferior caste of natural slaves seemed questionable.

It was largely due to the efforts of free blacks that whites, such as William Lloyd Garrison, began to argue against colonization as a racist ruse engineered to distract attention from the issue of emancipation. This opened the way, intellectually, to a push for the unconditional end of slavery: no period of preparation or apprenticeship before emancipation, and no forced emigration for freed slaves. "Treat us like men," the early black abolitionist David Walker wrote, "and there is no danger but we will all live in peace and happiness together."

American slavery was not headed toward extinction; it was a profitable enterprise that would not have died of natural causes. Davis thinks that if the South had somehow won or avoided the Civil War, slavery would have survived "well into the twentieth century." Most of the wealthiest Americans lived in the South in 1860, and as Walter Johnson has shown in his recent book *River of Dark Dreams* (2013), Southerners planned to expand their slaveholding empire into the Caribbean and Central America. If slavery was going to end, it had to be killed. The Thirteenth, Fourteenth and Fifteenth Amendments represent for Davis "the climax and turning point of the Age of Emancipation." By not only liberating but also granting citizenship and suffrage to some four million slaves, the amendments recognized the essential humanity of a previously dehumanized group. There were plenty of later steps backward, but this was still progress. "If my friends and I were suddenly stripped of our twentieth-century conditioning and plummeted back to Mississippi in 1860," he writes, "we would doubtless take for granted our rule over slaves. So an astonishing historical achievement really matters. The outlawing of chattel slavery in the New World, and then globally, represents a crucial landmark of moral progress that we should never forget."

Like much of Davis's later work, *Age of Emancipation* is hampered by an unevenness caused by lengthy digressions whose placement and purpose are clear only, perhaps, to their author. Yet the book's focus on dehumanization helps bring into sharp relief the centrality of that theme to the rest of Davis's career. The "psychological process" of dehumanization, he writes,

Kara Walker, *dread,* 2010

> deprives the dehumanized of those redeeming rational and spiritual qualities that give humans a sense of pride, of dignity, of being made in the image of God. At the same time, the projection enables the victimizers to become almost psychological parasites, whose self-image is immeasurably enhanced by the dramatic contrast with the degraded and dehumanized "Other." But why have we humans been so concerned with our "animality," and what is the ultimate source of this desire to animalize other humans—apart from the quite diverse motives of slaveholders, white supremacists, and Nazis? Here I would turn to Reinhold Niebuhr's view of the core of human "distinctiveness," as opposed to other animals, in the fear, self-doubt, anxiety, and even pride and confidence generated by the dilemma of finitude and freedom. ... If one samples some typical quotations on the human condition, we see a single answer in the tension between our sense of our existential animal finitude (evoked by our discovery in childhood that we are certain to die) and our capacity for self-reflection, for making ourselves our own object.

These are odd words for a historian, and it is easy to consider them extraneous to Davis's historical project. But in addition to reflecting the philosophical spirit that ensures Davis's work will continue to resonate with an audience far beyond his field, such passages describe both the depth and the ambition of that project. Informed by his experiences in the army and his intellectual encounter with Niebuhr, Davis grew attuned to the ways people try to become more than human by treating others as less than human. Niebuhr believed this to be a sin; and Davis has examined how modern society came to reject different sinful acts—homicide, enslavement—as possible paths to transcendence.

He sees his work as a historian as paving the way for another option. Ultimately, Davis comes back to the point he made in the letter he wrote to his parents from Germany, informing them that he would become a historian in order to "remember everything": that the real path to transcendence lies not in dehumanizing others but in understanding the past. "A consciousness of history," he has written, "is one of the key factors that distinguishes us from all other animals—I mean the ability to transcend an illusory sense of NOW, of an eternal present, and to strive for an understanding of the forces and events that made us what we are." The present, in other words, is a locked room to which history holds the key. To refuse to turn that key is to participate in our own dehumanization.

Liu Jianhua, *Unreal Scene*, 2008
All images courtesy of Galleria Continua

SEARCHING FOR SHANGHAI

NOTES FROM THE CITY OF THE FUTURE

by Moira Weigel

SOMETIMES SHANGHAI SEEMS to be everywhere. Late last September, on one of my first days back in New York after several months in China, I noticed a new sidewalk vending machine selling copies of *China Daily*, the English-language edition of the official Party newspaper. The headlines announced that Premier Li Keqiang had launched a bold economic experiment, persuading the State Council to create a Free Trade Zone (FTZ) in the city. There, foreign and private enterprises would invest freely and banks would convert yuan into and out of other currencies. Select Chinese companies would conduct offshore business, and goods would come and go without having to clear customs. The whole thing would occupy around eleven square miles.

The thumbnail map that ran beside the article showed a shaded polygon northeast of Pudong district, the glittering range of skyscrapers that looks over the older part of Shanghai from across the Huangpu River. It was labeled *Waigaoqiao*. The name means a "tall bridge outside," and I knew that there were many precedents for such an effort to bring in foreign business. Starting with the southern city of Shenzhen, in 1980, Deng Xiaoping created a series of Special Economic Zones along China's coast. The liberal economic policies and management practices that reigned there, as well as the government investment and tax incentives that these zones received, allowed them to play a key role in China's "reform and opening up." They attracted the foreign money that transformed an impoverished country into the "world's factory." They were why my childhood in Brooklyn in the 1990s was cluttered with objects made in the Pearl River Delta.

Nonetheless, after decades of dramatic development, China's economy had been stalling. In 2012 GDP growth was merely 7.8 percent—the lowest in thirteen years, since before China joined the WTO. Premier Li managed to create the FTZ because even skeptics within the Party leadership acknowledged that they needed another economic miracle. Shanghai makes sense as the place to look for it. The skyline built up in the past twenty years has often been cited as proof that the current leadership, whatever its other failings, can lift the country "from rice paddies to skyscrapers," fast.

China Daily opened its story on the FTZ by advertising the city's dramatic evolution. "Several decades of carefully planned development have transformed Shanghai from an industrial dinosaur filled with smokestacks into a modern service powerhouse adorned with gleaming high-rises full of banks, multinational enterprises, and large trading houses," the lede read. Like a time-lapse video in which the grubby "smokestacks" of bygone industry evaporate into merely metaphorical "powerhouses," this passage all but makes the city vanish. Yet despite being strangely bodiless, the place it conjures exerts a strong pull forward: "Shanghai has even grander things in store"; the FTZ is "a pilot project ... expected to pave the way"; a "test run ... widely seen as a precursor to economic restructuring and financial reform on a national level."

China Daily is, for obvious reasons, a paper that tends to present politics as a series of official decrees—statements about things that will happen and bring about other desirable ends. The banality of its optimism may be extreme. Yet as I read it in the New York subway, I realized that the sense of momentum it evoked is present in almost all rhetoric about China's development. That word, "development," itself conveys a strong sense of inevitability that the sci-fi resonances of words like "zone" intensify, as if the processes we hope for had merely to unfold. The press release spoke of Shanghai as if it represented a future—or, indeed, was already *in* that future, and would soon jolt the rest of the country into joining it there. I used to think about Shanghai that way, too.

THE FIRST TIME I went was basically by chance. It was my first time going anywhere in China. After one year of intensive Chinese courses at the university where I had started my Ph.D., I received a grant for a summer language-immersion program in Beijing. But I happened to have a month or so free before those classes began and nothing keeping me. I started looking for a project or pretext that would let me arrive early. It turned out that a more practical friend would be working at Shanghai's provincial sovereign wealth fund for the summer. At the time she seemed connected, capable; in retrospect, I suspect that she feared being lonely. In any case, she helped me apply for an internship at a television station owned by the Shanghai Media Group. And when her bosses confirmed they would be putting her up in a hotel suite, she offered me her extra bed.

In the hurried weeks before my departure, I read less than I had meant to. I did learn that historians dispute when Shanghai became Shanghai. The Chinese Communist Party commemorates 1291, the year in which Yuan Dynasty records first mention an administrative center on the Huangpu River. The true founding, however, has more often been dated to August 1842, when the British forced the Qing emperor to sign the treaty ending the first Opium War. The Treaty of Nanjing and the Treaty of the Bogue, which followed it in October 1843, created two foreign "concessions" around the old, walled "Chinatown": the International Concession, which was primarily British but also housed Americans, and the French Concession, which was French. Both were politically autonomous, with their own legal systems. They effectively opened the city to unlimited foreign settlement—there were few, if any, real controls on immigration—and to unrestricted trade.

In the boom years that followed, "shanghai" soon became a byword for misadventure. The OED cites the first use of the verb meaning "to enroll or obtain a sailor for the crew of a ship by unscrupulous means, as by liquor or drugging" to 1855. For decades the ratio of foreign men to women hovered around nine to one, hence the frontier-town atmosphere that made legends of women like the Sing Song Girls and the White Russian courtesan Shanghai Lily, whom Marlene Dietrich plays in Josef von Sternberg's *Shanghai Express* (1932). In another Sternberg noir, *The Shanghai Gesture* (1941), a Dragon Lady casino owner played by Ona Munson in yellowface stages a supposedly traditional Chinese New Year scene to titillate her foreign guests: a dozen girls in rags, of all races, are hoisted in bird cages above a crowd of slavering sailors who, she says, will bid to take them as sex slaves. The victims shriek as firecrackers erupt around them and the extras catcall below.

The extraterritorial status that made Shanghai infamously permissive inspired turn-of-the-century Chinese nationalists to see it as a place where anything might be possible. When the last Qing emperor stepped down, in 1911, it was to Shanghai that many patriotic intellectuals returned from abroad. After the Versailles Treaty turned over the German-occupied province of Shandong to Japan, the patriotic protest movements filled the streets, and the leaders began advocating the creation of literature in *baihua*, everyday speech; the polyglot journalist and later Party leader Qu Qiubai translated "L'Internationale" into vernacular Mandarin. The founding journals of the New Culture Movement, as it came to be called, moved to Beijing, but it was in a two-story house in Shanghai's French Concession that the Communist Party of China held their first

Liu Jianhua, *Unreal Scene*, 2008

congress in July 1921, with French and Russian advisors. Young Mao Zedong attended as the delegate from Hunan.

Mao and his army would put an end to the "century of humiliation" that the founding of modern Shanghai had begun. And yet, the sense of the city's exceptional status has persisted. Indeed, it has powerfully revived since the 1990s. As capital from the biggest economic boom in world history flowed in, and cultural producers followed, the city of the Chinese *internationale* reemerged as "global." A heady influx of migrant workers from the countryside, *waidiren*, helped build its iconic skyscrapers and boost its ranks: Shanghai is now the most populous city in the world. When Paris Hilton went to attend an MTV award show in 2007, she gushed that Shanghai "looks like the future" three times at a single press conference.

I **DID NOT NECESSARILY** expect to like it. But the idea of Shanghai began to exert a pull on me. As an American who has come of age in the era of what we are constantly told is our decline, I could not help feeling that Shanghai was on the right side of history—and feel drawn to a momentum that I hoped would touch and somehow change me.

In fact, from the moment of my arrival, I experienced the city as a series of almost continual frustrations and delays.

When I finished the thirty-hour concatenation of flights that I booked from Newark via London, I realized that I had failed to write down my hotel address. At the exit from the airport terminal, a hustler in a tulip skirt, who must have been stationed to scan the curb for just such occasions, saw me struggling to tell a cab driver where I thought it was. She snatched my Google Maps printout, marched me inside to make some calls, and then back out to her guy, lugging my club-footed duffle bag in one stinging hand. She charged me 500 yuan, something like 80 USD, at least three times what it should be.

From the ride, I remember the moment when the white cords of the Huangpu Bridge soared into view to our right, above the river, gold with sunning filth, and we turned west, following the first ring road down into a series of arcing, leafy streets. At an intersection where our car stopped at a red light, I saw a fruit seller stooping to yoke his neck into a carrying pole, cross the street, and continue into the shade, his two heaped baskets swaying in tempo with his step. The driver told me a long story, the punchline to which I had look up: *jiaguji*, "jacuzzi."

My friend's suite turned out to be a single room with one desk and a fridge too small to hold the bottle of Sprite I had bought at Heathrow in any posture. The hotel was run by the Party, and notwithstanding its location at the north edge of the former French Concession, and the Muzak rendering of "Non, je ne regrette rien" that sometimes tinkled in the elevators, I never saw another foreigner there. Before opening my VPN to log in to Facebook, which crashed our dial-up for the afternoon, I wrote emails saying I had arrived smoothly and that Shanghai looked great. It did. The city's scale and strangeness made even trivial mishaps interesting.

My second day, spent finding my way to a jangling electronics mall called Metro City, did not feel like a waste, even though I failed to find someone to unlock my iPhone. The salesgirl who finally sold me the same model Nokia that I had used as a foreign student in Berlin in 2005 trailed me for an hour, practicing her English by bitching about her Egyptian boyfriend. He would not marry her because of his religion. "In Shanghai," she warned me, "foreign men just want to *float*." Did she mean *swing*?

The solecisms that I ran into around the city were giving me a pretty good idea of what my Chinese must have sounded like, at best. During my first days in Shanghai, phrases I had carefully memorized kept tripping all wrong off my lips. I misheard the proprietor of a bakery politely saying hello (*ni chi gou le*) for his exclaiming in surprise that I liked dog meat (*ni chi gou ah!*) and spat a mouthful of harmless veggie bun out into my palm. I had been meticulous asking a waitress for tofu, since a teacher had once warned me that if I fumbled my word order I would say something risqué. But tacking a Sprite (*xuebi*) on to the end of my order in the wrong tone I inadvertently asked for "and one snow-cunt!"

That night, my friend and I took the first of what would become habitual walks—three, even four miles east, under the humming Ring Road. We went as far as Jing'an Temple and the maze of shops around it. We stopped in side streets, lingered at food stalls hissing with hunks of smarting meat, and then headed on toward the Miu Miu and Gucci billboards that marked People's Square. As we wandered, the abstractions with which I had arrived, the idea of the city as a shiny thing of glass and steel, began to dissolve into concrete details.

In the alleys behind the lane houses, strings of ghostly laundry hung, drying, beneath windows lit like north stars. In larger avenues, food vendors set up noodle stands, and people sat at low plastic tables, smoking and playing cards past midnight. All kinds of things were for sale. Men on bicycles pedaled barges stacked with densely packed plastic recycling, or with pastel mountains of plush teddy bears. Peddlers set up carts with heaps of dishware or stacks of pirated books and DVDs. For some reason, all of them seemed to be playing either "Bés-

ame Mucho" or "The Wind Beneath My Wings." The godmother who babysat me when I was a child used to watch the Bette Midler movie that song comes from, and hum the tune, but until then I would have sworn I had forgotten.

I HAD EXPECTED DAYS at the TV station to move faster. Having been invited to help out on a lifestyle show called *City Beat*, I went in with aspirations to work hard and sniff out the true story of how state-owned media functioned. But as it turned out I spent much of every day at my desk, attempting to look occupied. By day three, boredom had given me the courage to sneak one of the few paperbacks that I had brought with me to China out from my Longchamp purse. André Malraux's *Man's Fate* was already wilting in the wet May heat. I curled it open in my lap and read.

Published in 1933, *Man's Fate* centers on a failed Communist uprising that took place in 1927 and led to what is called the "April 12th incident," "purge," "counterrevolutionary coup," "tragedy" or "massacre," depending on whom you ask. In March of that year, Zhou Enlai led a force of union workers to defeat the warlords then controlling the city. They occupied and governed the Chinese districts for weeks before the National Revolutionary Army arrived, at the invitation of the European powers the Nationalists were hoping to replace. Chiang Kai-shek declared martial law and issued a secret order to expel all Communists from the Kuomintang (KMT). When thousands of students and union members went to his army to protest, soldiers opened fire, killing one hundred and wounding more. Zhou fled to Wuhan, and the young Mao to the countryside, where the violent course that the twentieth century would take began.

Malraux tells the story of the uprising through the fictional, French-Japanese leader Kyo Gisors, and the Chinese assassin T'chen. The novel was a runaway bestseller and won the Prix Goncourt in Popular Front Paris. The great Soviet director Sergei Eisenstein so admired it that when Malraux came to attend the First Writer's Congress in Moscow, he locked both of them in a room for days, to write an adaptation that never materialized.

The next morning, I emailed in sick. I swiped a few *mantou* (steamed buns) and satchels of jam from the hotel breakfast buffet and lay in bed reading until afternoon. Outside, the cathedral arch the plane trees made above the curving streets of the concession bent in the wind. It was going to rain. A woman selling lychees stood up, fit the balance over her neck, then started making her way toward Fuxing Lu. When the *fuwuyuan* came in to change the sheets and found me still in them she looked at me with what seemed like embarrassment. I accepted two bottled waters and told her she did not need to make my bed.

IN *MAN'S FATE*, all but the most cynical characters die in the end. But at the time Malraux was writing, other visitors to Shanghai were offering brighter visions. A 1934 travel guide that I came across, quoted in a history book, called it "Paris of the East! The New York of the West! The most cosmopolitan city in the world ... a vast brilliantly hued cycloramic, panoramic mural of the best and worst of Orient and Occident!" When Christopher Isherwood and his friend and sometimes lover W. H. Auden traveled across China by train to research the travel book they were to write together, *Journey to a War* (1939), Shanghai was where they chose to finish. Isherwood makes the city sound like a genie lamp that lets you wish for more wishes:

> You can buy an electric razor or a French dinner, or a well-cut suit. You can dance at the Tower Restaurant on the roof of the Cathay Hotel, and gossip with Freddy Kaufmann, its charming manager, about the European aristocracy of pre-Hitler Berlin. You can attend race-meetings, baseball games, football matches. You can see the latest American films. If you want girls, or boys, you can have them, at all prices, in the bath-houses and brothels. If you want opium you can smoke it in the best company, served on a tray, like afternoon tea ... Finally, if you ever repent, there are churches and chapels of all denominations.

The next generation of European aesthetes remained attracted to Shanghai, but they went looking for something different: not the worldly pleasure park that Isherwood had sought out, but proof that a *cultural* revolution could live up to its promise to transform society. Roland Barthes came in 1974 as one of a group of French Maoists from the literary journal *Tel Quel*, invited by Mao's government under the supervision of the official Travel Bureau. (Jacques Lacan was also supposed to go, but pulled out at the last minute.) Barthes had been writing prolifically about his travels in Japan since the 1960s and hoped that the trip would produce a book. But what he came up with was only a brief article in *Le Monde* entitled "Alors, la Chine?"

It is the record of a disappointment. "We went to China armed with a thousand pressing and, it seemed, natural questions," Barthes writes. "We shook the tree of knowledge in order to make it answer, so that we could return supplied with what is our primary intellectual nourishment: a secret deciphered. But nothing fell. In a sense, other than the political answers we received, we returned with nothing." It was not until 2009 that a fuller account of Barthes' travels in China appeared: the three notebooks that he filled over the course of the three-week trip.

Barthes knew from the beginning that describing the country would be a struggle, and he soon got sick of rehearsed speeches. On a scheduled visit to a worker's home, Barthes writes: "Set theme of Gratitude. Set theme Past/Present. [Here: Theme of the Poor.]" When his wife speaks: "She develops the Set Theme, with personal incidents ... [The Story, the Repetition, the lesson: the *lectio*.] [Rising anti-stereotype nausea.]"

Unlike Malraux or Isherwood, Barthes spends a lot of time seeing himself being seen. He recalls getting gawked at in the Nanjing Zoo. "Double zoo: we stare at the Panda, fifty people stare at us." China itself keeps startling Barthes by looking and sounding familiar: "One peacock cries 'Léon Léon'..." On his first day in Shanghai he notices "three women of three different ages washing clothes in a wooden tub, with a plank like in Morocco." He sees French friends in Chinese faces—"an emaciated writer in his cap, who reminds me of Foucault." He concludes that as a fact-finding mission the *Tel Quel* trip is hopeless. "I feel that I won't be able to shed light on them in the least ... just shed light on us by means of them." He concludes: "What needs to be written isn't *So, what about China?*, but *So, what about France?*"

BARTHES RECOGNIZED THAT what *Tel Quel* was looking for in Mao's China was a mirage. Where Malraux had wanted to create an imaginary history by documenting an urban revolution that never took place, the French Maoists wanted evidence that the radical aesthetic principles that they had been promoting in Paris could help bring about a revolution in consciousness—or, as the Chairman had put it, a "systematic remolding of human minds." Indeed, the fictions about Shanghai that I misspent my time in the city reading gradually showed me how powerful this city was *as* a fiction. The power of this fiction has drawn successive generations of visitors to rewrite it, each in the image of their own desires.

So what about us?

The truth is that the foreigners I met in Shanghai mostly wanted to party. (Barthes himself conceded that the Shanghai streets would be "good for cruising." "A lot of people, more attractive!" he jots in his notebooks as soon as the plane bearing the *Tel Quel* contingent lands.) The friend who was hosting me in her hotel valiantly found friends of friends, even of friends of friends, who lived in Shanghai. Most seemed to be finance guys, or diplobrats who had stayed after their parents left, or kids who had bungled university in Britain or France, convinced their father or uncle to buy them a one-way ticket, and were now killing it with the Ferrari contract, with the Lancôme contract, with the TAG Heuer contract. I made friends, too. Between our efforts, we went somewhere almost every night.

We went to Ladies Night at the clubs on Yongufulu, accepted free champagne flutes and, at the servers' insistence, cardboard party hats. We met a lanky Australian named Brad who had just moved to Shanghai to work for Tesco when he leaped into the open door of our cab, a sausage-truck sausage still in hand, and redirected it to another club called Velvet, where he bought a $300 bottle that no one touched.

We went to a dinner party hosted by a woman who designed BDSM-inspired shoes at the apartment she had built for herself above her studio and cooed, with everyone, over the portraits of her pug that she had hired local graffiti artists to cover the walls with. The real pug, outfitted in a Bottega Veneta collar, trotted beneath the table—which consisted of a slab of glass balanced on a thicket of interlocking mannequin legs clad in bright stockings and that season's line of footwear. Over dinner, ruddy businessmen talked about how China was "over"; they were planning to move on to Burma next year.

We went to the party that a fashion blogger who was "famous on Weibo" (Chinese Twitter) held in his boutique-hotel suite in honor of a new lifestyle magazine that he was launching. We ate almonds and goaded two brothers who said they were doing a project on urban spaces and utopia, but who seemed to make their living as consultants, into lifting their polo shirts far enough to show us the matching Lacoste alligators they claimed to have tattooed onto their left pectorals. They did (and they did).

We went to a lecture at a new museum aimed at prospective donors and their impeccable wives, given by a French curator with bleached hair, white jeans and a visible crotch bulge. He pontificated for two hours about the history of the museum since the French Revolution, then showed a video of anime Minotaurs copulating as an example of what kind of work he, as curator, would bring to this space. When the others clapped, we clapped.

We went on, justifying our exhaustion on the grounds that a rush was what we had come for. In its current incarnation, Shanghai has superficially revived the anything-goes "phantasmagoria" that Isherwood described in the 1930s. Indeed, in rebranding the city as a hub of global capital, the contemporary Party

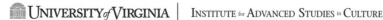

leadership has embraced and reclaimed precisely the cosmopolitan—colonial—history that the Maoists aimed to destroy. It is as if nothing has changed, in the half century that this version of the story rather willfully elides; at the same time, everything has.

Foreigners have always come to Shanghai in order to feel that they are living on the verge of the future. For Malraux, that future was Communist. For *Tel Quel*, it was peopled by new kinds of social collectives, thinking and speaking in fresh, new languages. Today, foreigners travel to Shanghai because they believe that China will be the world's next economic superpower. The city serves as a beacon of hypercapitalism that, it seems to promise, will survive the global financial crisis, beyond the reach of politics and even geography.

All of these visions are utopian; and as utopias, they feel curiously placeless. And yet the sense of placelessness that repeatedly invades the Pudong district, and which places like the Waigaoqiao FTZ seem designed to epitomize, comes from a very specific place. The future that they conjure has a very particular history. Thinking about Shanghai and its prospects now, I can't help but remember the pantheon of past visitors to whom my own procrastination reading introduced me. The futures that drew them never arrived. Or, rather, when the time came, Shanghai was never quite as they had imagined.

Bjarke Ingels, from *Yes is More*, 2009

BUILDING STORIES

HOW COMICS CAN CURE ARCHITECTURE

by Merve Emre *and* Christian Nakarado

LAST NOVEMBER, KANYE WEST stopped by Harvard University's Graduate School of Design to deliver a three-minute manifesto on the state of architecture today. Standing atop a drafting table in the middle of the school's cavernous design studio, impeccably turned out in a white bomber jacket and faux construction boots, Kanye issued a series of proclamations on creativity unbound. "I really do believe that the world can be saved through design and everything can be architected," he announced to his cheering audience. "I believe," he continued, "that utopia is actually possible—but we're led by the least noble, the least dignified, the least tasteful, the dumbest and the most political." In a world cluttered by artistic and intellectual detritus, the architect's studio emerged as one of the only free spaces for utopian thought. Here the imagination could run wild, unbridled by such constraints as money, politics, bad taste and the desires of other human beings. For Kanye, the fantasy of total self-creation was nothing short of revolutionary. He concluded on an uncharacteristically humble note: "I'm very inspired to be in this space."

Say what you will about Kanye West's edifice complex, but he's not the first person to suggest that we can build our way to "utopia"—a term as imprecise as it is overused in architectural theory. When Kanye talks about utopia, he is not holding up a generally "virtuous" or "just" way of building, à la utopia's master theorists like Plato or Sir Thomas More. Rather, Kanye is pulling from an overstuffed grab bag of design principles that have served as the keystones of the twentieth century's major architectural movements. The futuristic pavilions of communism dreamed up by the Soviet Union's constructivist architects in the 1920s and 1930s were pitched as everyday utopian spaces for the masses. The rational modernism of the 1940s and 1950s claimed as utopian those buildings that reflected the material conditions of mid-century industrialism—single-family homes made entirely of steel and glass and reinforced concrete, like Le Corbusier's Villa Savoye or Mies van der Rohe's Farnsworth House. Even the fragmented follies of Bernard Tschumi's Parc de la Villette in 1982 were presented as a postmodern utopia, the ideal reflection of how late capitalism had resulted in total spatial disintegration. For much of the last century, then, laying claim to utopia, in theory and in practice, was the most compelling strategy for announcing a new direction in design.

But since the 1980s, we have seen a decoupling of utopian language, however vague or slipshod it may seem, from actual building practices. In no small part, this is due to the rise of commercial "starchitects" like Norman Foster and Frank Gehry, happy to recycle last year's designs for billionaire developers who are, in turn, happy to look the other way as creativity grinds to a halt. Bored by what commercial design has to offer, utopian thought and experimental design have retreated to the academy. There it keeps company with theoretical architects like Tschumi, John Hejduk and Peter Eisenman, who rose to prominence in the 1980s and 1990s only to be pushed to the margins of commercial practice. These "paper architects" of the avant-garde—so called because they work exclusively in the medium of drawing—are the last holdouts of a creative impulse that has lost its way to the real world. So the question remains: After the schism of building in theory and building in practice, what hope is there for a reunion of imagination and concrete?

Kanye thinks he has the answer. So does Bjarke Ingels, the architecture world's own enfant terrible and rising starchitect of the moment. Some will recognize Ingels as the heir apparent to Rem Koolhaas, founder of OMA and arguably the most controversial architect of the last thirty years—not to mention one of Kanye's recent design collaborators. Others may recall Ingels from the lengthy profile that appeared in the *New Yorker* late last year, just as he was preparing to break ground on his first project in New York City: a slick white pyramid that will soon slice through W. 57th St., known around town simply as "W57." But several years before he became a household name in New York, Ingels's Copenhagen-based practice, Bjarke Ingels Group (BIG), wrote and illustrated *Yes Is More*, a 400-page comic book that BIG marketed as a "manifesto of pop culture." In it, Ingels and his team use BIG's designs to make the case for architecture as a practice of "pragmatic utopianism"—a utopia that is actually possible—while loudly championing Ingels as the master architect of our future.

Ingels peddles a utopia of total creative control. *Yes Is More* imagines cities in which perfectly identical buildings can be stacked on top of one another like Legoland sets, encouraging city blocks skyward, one module at a time. It

Yakov Chernikov, *Giant Plant of Special Purpose*, 1931

Mies van der Rohe, *Farnsworth House*, 1951

Bernard Tschumi, *Parc de la Villette*, 1982-88

transforms quiet waterfronts into "super-harbors" that teem with shipping containers and trade traffic; we can imagine how the logos of DONDA—Kanye's newly established design practice—or BIG might bask proudly in the sunlight that shines off the water. In *Yes Is More*, residences, offices and shopping malls proudly merge in urban monoliths with names like "Bureaucratic Beauty" or "Infinity Loop"—a hard-to-miss suggestion that these buildings are designed to ensure that every aspect of public and private life is lived in "total compliance" with the architect's vision of the future. This is the twisted fantasy whose popular diffusion links W. 57th St. to Kanye West, and utopia to the depersonalized designs that are currently infiltrating our cities.

While Ingels's design aesthetic lacks space for even the most basic varieties of humanity, his turn to the comic book form with *Yes Is More* is nevertheless telling. For one, the architect's foray into the world of comics shows us why the comic form is so well suited for thinking about—and drawing—utopia. As John McMorrough writes in his introduction to Chicago-area architect Jimenez Lai's graphic novel *Citizens of No Place*, comic book artists use space to create "pocket universes where possibility is unregulated by the weight of history or, in some cases, even the weight of gravity." (Lai takes this directive quite literally by designing a utopian spaceship that bears an uncanny resemblance to the luxury cruise liner from Pixar's *WALL-E*.) Like Kanye's fantasy of the architect's studio, the comic can offer a narrative supplement to real buildings—a different form of "paper architecture," keenly attuned to the construction of new, experimental worlds.

But if the comic form can illuminate the experimental possibilities of architecture, it can just as easily expose its limitations, throwing into relief the shallowness of a design concept, say, or its sloppy articulation. In making the impossible banal, *Yes Is More* falls prey to precisely this kind of self-exposure. The comic's heavy lines and bright colors exacerbate Ingels's penchant for flatness, yielding cartoon structures so dense and impenetrable that they stop the imagination. The speech and thought bubbles that allow Ingels to narrate BIG's triumph over unsuspecting landscapes and funding impasses contain language best reserved for the comic-book villain. "We architects don't have to remain misunderstood geniuses, frustrated by the lack of understanding, appreciation or funding," he announces in the manifesto's opening pages. In reading *Yes Is More*, one thinks not of Rem Koolhaas's manifesto *Delirious New York* but of graphic novelist Chip Kidd's *Batman: Death by Design*, which casts as Batman's nemesis a preening architect named Kem Roomhaus, hell-bent on transforming Gotham City according to his garishly outsize tastes. Big is bad for mankind.

Despite the expansive arrogance of *Yes Is More*, there is something playful and compelling about the idea that comics can breathe new life into contemporary architecture. What if we flipped the relationship between architecture and the comic on its head? What if we asked how professional comic artists have chosen to visualize the future of architectural design? Where the architect's imagination has floundered, works of comic art like David Mazzucchelli's *Asterios Polyp* and Chris Ware's *Building Stories* have emerged as superior examples of paper architecture, buoyed by similar questions about how we inhabit space. Where the architectural comic has gone big in order to grapple with its utopian impulses, comic art has gone small. By small, we don't mean diminutive in stature or modest in ambition. Rather, the small and supple worlds of comic art feature built spaces we can navigate and construct with our hands, bringing us one step closer to the experience of touching—and feeling intimately in touch with—our dwellings.

AT THE CROSSROADS of architecture and the comic is Mazzucchelli's *Asterios Polyp*, the love story of architecture professor Asterios Polyp—an unwieldy, snobbish, weak-chinned scrap of a man—and his lovely wife Hana. Asterios is one of the paper architects of the 1980s and 1990s avant-garde, a tight-knit coterie of poststructuralist designers who took their cues directly from French philosopher Jacques Derrida's understanding of architecture as a form of writing. Like Derrida's one-time collaborator Peter Eisenman, Asterios's reputation rests on "his designs, rather than on the buildings constructed from them." Nothing he has designed has ever been built. Rather, his career is an accumulation of riddles, abstractions and analogues, systems and sequences "governed by their own internal logic." They take little by way of inspiration from the material world and give next to nothing back. *Asterios Polyp*, we could conclude, is the story of a man who could have authored a savvier version of *Yes Is More*.

Mazzucchelli draws Asterios as an extension of his intellectual sensibilities, a not-so-subtle takedown of architectural theory that's delightful to behold in comic form. At his most pedantic moments—lecturing a class on Apollonian versus Dionysian design, or boasting about his sexual prowess at a faculty meeting—Asterios's body morphs into an artist's mannequin, a cool blue assemblage of hollow geometries that bear no relationship to the world around him. Meeting Hana for the first time, his form fills out. She is all warmth and feeling, a shy sculptor who enters Asterios's life in hundreds of delicate pink brushstrokes, like one of Toulouse-Lautrec's barstool muses but with infinitely less self-assurance. Hana makes messy and inviting sculptures out of found objects. She reveres the imperfect shapes of half-plucked daisies and pine cones and knitting loops; her medium is garbage. When she and Asterios meet, their coupling is the stuff of myth—Aristophanes's long-lost soul mates completing each other, aesthetically and emotionally.

But like most mythic couples, their love falls prey to hubris. After all, Asterios was the birth name of the Minotaur, an unlovable monster trapped by Daedalus's labyrinthine take on a simple design problem. Asterios does not see how the idea of utopia—in design and, by extension, in love—can hem in the imagination until there's room left for only one person's construction of the rules of art and life. Asterios's narcissism, we are meant to believe, is intimately connected to his inflexible aesthetic beliefs—"the certitude of symmetry, the consonance of counterpoise" and the "eloquent equilibriums" that inspire his impossible-to-build designs. He holds on to these beliefs at great cost. Hana divorces him fiercely and suddenly, leaving Asterios to grieve in a labyrinth of his own making.

Like most tragic heroes, Asterios is given the chance to redeem himself. After a fire destroys his New York apartment, Asterios takes a despairing bus ride into the heart of Middle America—the East Coast academic's descent into the underworld. There, in a small town named Apogee, he finds a job as a car repairman, working for a burly auto mechanic named Stiff Major and living with Stiff's family, his clairvoyant wife Ursula Major and their son Jackson. Stripped of his pretensions and worldly possessions—the Breuer chairs, the van der Rohe lounge—Asterios begins to build. Out of a pile of reclaimed wood, he and Stiff decide to make a tree house for Jackson. "I'm no Frank Lord Wright," Stiff claims as he thrusts a crumpled piece of paper at Asterios, "but I made a little sketch."

Ironically, it does look a little like one of Frank Lloyd Wright's houses, a modest tip of the hat to Fallingwater and its intimate rapport with nature. Nestled in the treetops, its roof cantilevering out over the boughs, the tree house is Asterios's first construction, a collaborative effort between Stiff's design and Asterios's own two hands. Mazzucchelli pays special attention to these hands when drawing the construction process. We see them palming the planks as if to test their firmness; we see jolts of energy—normally reserved for the comic book's "ZAP!" "BAM!" or "POW!" moments—that connect the hammer in Asterios's left hand to the nail in his right; we see the sinuous tensing in his forearms as he grips at the rope that binds the planks to the tree, reuniting the discarded wood with the nature whence it came. From building comes a different way of being and—literally—of being in touch with the world, one that trades the siren song of utopia for the smaller delights of handicraft. Only now can Asterios return to Hana, armed with an appreciation for working together to build something that endures. Only now can she forgive him.

David Mazzucchelli, from *Asterios Polyp*, 2009

From *Asterios Polyp*, we could go back to architectural theory—to Martin Heidegger, author of the slim and intractable essay "Building Dwelling Thinking," which considers the world-making powers of built space; or Emmanuel Petit, who in a recent issue of *Log* celebrates the possibility of a sensual, even organismic closeness between people and interiors. But it is more illuminating to connect the devotional handicraft of *Asterios Polyp* to architects who have paid homage to the human hand in practice, like Pierre Chareau, William Morris, or, more recently, Tom Kundig. Chareau's most famous commission, the Maison de Verre, may seem more sophisticated than Asterios's tree house—it was once the preferred meeting place of Walter Benjamin and Jean Cocteau in Paris—but its design honors similar principles. Every corner is nimbly packed with gadgets and gizmos: spinning gears, rotating levers, extendable hinges and pivoting surfaces whose kinetic essence encourages or even demands their obsessive use. Here the hand is key. By touching, turning, pressing and pulling on skylights and walls, one can alter the parts of the house that are crucial to its design, thereby participating in its authorship. Far removed from the architect of utopia, who lords over an unreal city, the shared human touch is what makes building—and buildings—desirable, now and into the ever-shifting future.

PERHAPS NO RECENT work of comic art has enjoyed as much praise from readers and illustrators alike as Chris Ware's *Building Stories*. Reviewing it, Daniel Worden speaks of Ware's architectural "nostalgia for an earlier industrial era," and compares the Chicago brownstone that sits at the center of *Building Stories* to "a ruin"—an "aesthetic object" that elicits "melancholy" for the irrecoverable past. Indeed, Ware's tale of an unnamed woman overcome by depression, anxiety, self-doubt and ennui sprawls masterfully across fourteen pieces of text—a handful of books both large and small, newspaper pullouts, pamphlets, even a board game. It also covers nearly one hundred years in the life of a Humboldt Park brownstone, one that has succumbed to the kind of shabby gentility that precedes demolition. But for most readers, unused to spending this much time with a building, poring over the thousands of angles from which Ware has chosen to draw it, *Building Stories* exudes an immediacy that the ruin denies. Like *Asterios Polyp*, it extends the promise of shared creation: by touching and turning and arranging the pieces of *Building Stories*, you can build your own story, inhabit your own intimately knowable and narrateable world.

Ware has claimed that architecture is "the aesthetic key to the development of the cartoons as an art form." (Ware's notebooks and sketches from the past two decades are chock-full of statements like this.) But we could just as easily flip his observation, and claim that *Building Stories*' intimate sense of touch unlocks radical ways of sensing buildings—as conscious, powerful and motivated; buildings as not merely aesthetic objects, but subjects unto themselves. In *Building Stories*, the building narrates its own history in a fusty, cursive hand that trails in and out of its rooms like an absentminded great aunt, pausing here and there to run a finger over a pair of dusty end tables and reminisce. "It relied on the memory of tenants to stay alive," the building thinks of itself, as it sheds a shingle to mourn the memories of tenants past:

> It particularly preferred the company of the younger women—(They usually did such tasteful things with the place, kept it clean...)
>
> Plus the pink pitter-patter of freshly showered feet, tickling its joints... that was always nice.
>
> Actually, there were a number of good memories... What was her name? She liked to roll around on the floor...
>
> Or this one... a bit fat, but she had friendly fingers and a warm rump...
>
> Or her—the way she'd open a door; gently grasp, twist, and pull... oh!

Buried in these recollections is a serious provocation: If you tickle us, do we not laugh? Where it once seemed impossible for fiction to imagine the inner states of human beings dissimilar to us, Ware dares us to embody the consciousness of something nonhuman and, in doing so, to consider our incommensurable senses of touch. If you were a building, what would it feel like to have your joints tickled? Your knobs twisted? How might you experience the weight and warmth of the human body, its cleanliness and color? Is this building's lingering "oh!" a cry of pleasure or pain or something else entirely? Is it a sensation that we cannot reroute by way of our all-too-human metaphors?

We could interpret Ware's provocation to imagine how a building feels on its own terms as radically severing *Building Stories* from the human point of view. But Ware's building is never entirely separate from the consciousness of the building's third-floor tenant, the unnamed woman who lost her left leg in a motorboat accident. Pink-cheeked, a little dowdy, depression-prone and unshakably lonely, she is most often seen hobbling from room to room, wondering what to do with her life. Over time, her body and thoughts seem to map the building's interior spaces. "Having spent an unusual amount of my childhood sitting on

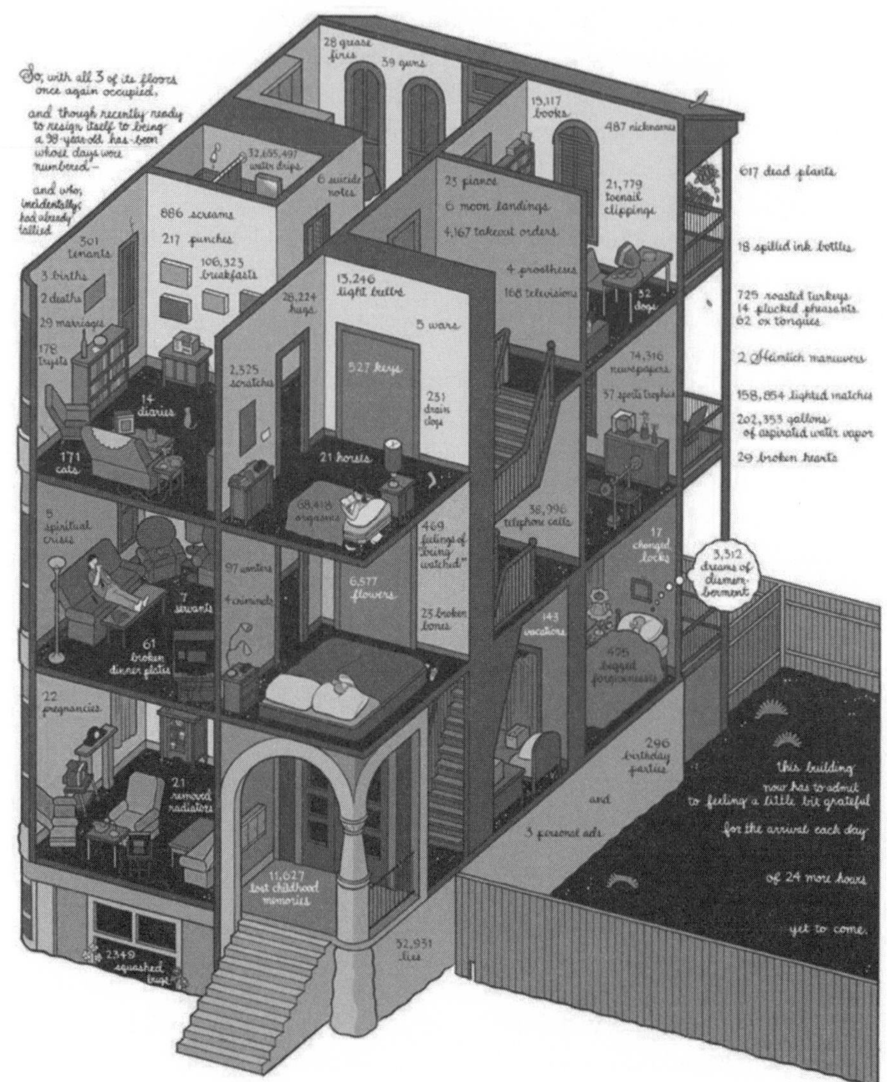

Chris Ware, from *Building Stories*, 2012

the floor," she writes in her diary, "I became more than a little acquainted with the world of baseboards, doorstops and electrical plugs, to say nothing of all the valves and faucets that hide behind toilets and sinks." In a moment that recalls Chareau's house of gadgets, she confronts an overflowing toilet with her crutch—an extension of her body—plugging it into the toilet's fill valve to stop the water from running. "I was sort of proud of myself for figuring this out," she confesses, "You just don't realize how much you take things for granted until they're taken away ... how interdependent the 'modern' world is." It is the interdependence between humans and buildings—the fusion of the tactile with the tectonic—that provides the woman a rare break from her numb resignation. No matter how sad or small this connectivity might seem, it is one of the only ways for her to be and to feel in relation to the world.

Today the house of fiction is full of such "alien phenomenologies," to borrow a term from critic and graphic designer Ian Bogost. But Ware suggests that they are largely absent from the esteemed buildings of American architecture, whose imaginative possibilities seem foreclosed by their iconicity. In one of *Building Stories*' newspaper-sized pamphlets, Ware airlifts his readers from Humboldt Park to Oak Park, the leafy suburb that is home to many of Frank Lloyd Wright's early homes, including the Frank Lloyd Wright Home and Studio. (Built in 1889 with a loan from his employer Louis Sullivan, the Wright Home effectively launched the career that would dwarf Sullivan's own by the next decade.) A century later, Ware's unnamed woman walks down the streets of Oak Park huffing at the Wright Home's status as a mere "tourist attraction." Against the vibrant greens of springtime, there it sits, a flat and uninviting slab of art. "Sometimes I really hate it here," the woman thinks as she pushes past the horde of gawping German tourists who clog the sidewalk. The tourists need to be reminded that "people still live and work" around these parts, but it's not entirely their fault. In becoming iconic and therefore uninhabitable, the Wright House has forsaken its contact with the life of the imagination. It can no longer offer the kinds of in-touch experiences that the brownstone delights in. (We could say the same of any contemporary architect who aims to fix an icon, rather than create a space for dwelling.)

For Ware, there is a radical and touching interdependence between humans and things, designers and dwellers, form and everyday function. "Not to brag, but we buildings are able to—how might you say it—grope our way around the future a bit," the brownstone announces, groping its way to a prophecy: its lonely tenant will marry a young architect whom she meets at a friend's party and invites up to her apartment one evening in an act of unprecedented bravery, leaving the building vacant and alone. Eventually the bulldozers and wrecking

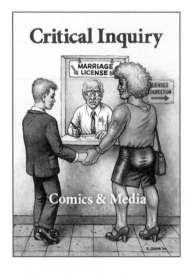

balls will come for it. But it will not be gone—at least, not entirely. In what could be considered one of the strangest panels in *Building Stories*, Ware flashes forward 150 years to a man and a woman standing where the building had once stood, their heads encased by a virtual interface that is busy pulling "memory fragments" from "this area's consciousness cloud." As they read the building's memories, visualizing its inhabitants and recording their feelings, the woman reflects on the self-centeredness that once obscured from human beings the truth about our existence. "People really did think they were just single particles back then," she observes in disbelief.

Against the ego and narcissism of big utopia, against its desire for absolute control, the paper architecture of graphic novels gives us a simple alternative: let us grope our way into the interdependent future—one small, delightful touch at a time.

Jules de Balincourt, *Poor Planning*, 2005

MOBILIZING MUTUAL LEARNING

BUREAUCRACY AND IDEALISM IN TARTU, ESTONIA

by Jonny Thakkar

A LITTLE OVER TWO weeks before the final draft of my Ph.D. was due to be submitted to the University of Chicago library, I found myself in a windowless room above a big-box shopping center in southern Estonia holding hands with a circle of strangers. The dissertation, which concerned the harmony of wholes and parts, was a mess. Reading from start to finish a few days earlier had been a shock. It was all over the place stylistically; the topic kept changing; whole swathes needed to be cut. But I had contracted to go to Estonia—and, I said to myself, it might be good for me.

The call had come out of nowhere. A long-lost friend—we had been out of contact for eleven and a half years, having spent six months of a "gap year" teaching together in the countryside of Lesotho—messaged me on Facebook apologizing in advance for the ludicrous proposal he was about to make. He was working for the University of Liverpool, he explained, on a project to involve children in decisions about science education. The project was based in Liverpool but sponsored by the European Commission and it had several European partners. The next conference was to be in an Estonian town called Tartu and my friend's boss had had the idea of sponsoring innovative reflections on its proceedings: she was looking for a video artist, a poet and an essayist. Might I be interested in speaking to her?

It didn't seem all that promising. The academic conferences I had experienced were mostly fraudulent to their core, CV-building and networking exercises masquerading as intellectual symposia. And even if this were to be an earnest attempt to listen and learn, would it really provide me enough material for an essay? There was a huge difference between the reportage I guessed they were looking for and the sort of philosophical and cultural criticism I was used to producing. Assuming I stuck to the latter, the situation was potentially awkward. Was it unethical to accept a commission from the object of one's critique? Or just embarrassing? In any case, I was busy. Still, it seemed impolite not to at least hear the proposal, and so like a good Englishman I buttoned up my doubts and shuffled sheepishly into a Skype conversation.

Tricia Jenkins, "principal investigator" of the project in question, turned out to be, as my mother would say, "quite a character." A somewhat hippie-ish lady with a shock of frizzy blond hair, verging on retirement age, she talked rapidly and insistently; behind her hung a brown drape featuring silhouettes of what looked to be a series of exotic dancers, possibly African. When I asked her to explain what she was doing and what she was looking for, she began, surprisingly, by telling me about the process of getting funding from the European Commission. What followed was somewhat mysterious to me—something about needing at least ten different entities with ten different legal statuses from ten different countries before being able to go through the relevant supranational "frameworks," "silos" and "directorates," and something about the whole thing depending on whether one was aiming at "delivery" or at "mobilizing mutual learning"—but in any case it soon became clear that "process" may be the wrong word, as opposed to, say, "art" or "alchemy" or, to put it more bluntly, "profession." For so complex is the whole process, Tricia explained, that funding tends to be secured only by experts in securing funding, with the result that most new projects are run by the same people who ran the old projects. Thankfully, twenty-eight years working on a variety of European projects at the University of Liverpool had brought Tricia herself some of this expertise—and the lavishly funded project for whose sake the Tartu conference was to be organized, "SiS Catalyst," was to be her last hurrah before riding off into a South American retirement.

The basic idea of SiS Catalyst, Tricia explained, was to get children from disadvantaged backgrounds into science. If there are disproportionately few black doctors in the U.K., for example, this is because there are disproportionately few black applicants to medicine courses, and this in turn has to do with culture rather than ability. What is needed is a shift in expectations, and SiS Catalyst was trying to effect this by piggybacking on some Austrian initiatives to interest children in science via so-called "children's universities"—open days or outreach sessions in which universities put on classes for children. This aspiration is obviously highly commendable, but what was more appealing from the perspective of having to write an essay, truth be told, was the jargon in which it was clad.

"Change occurs through individuals," Tricia told me, and these individuals are "change agents." In this case, change agents meant children and current students but also "key players," a category comprising policy-makers, journalists, "locally defined enablers" (e.g. teachers) and "operational key players," of whom Tricia herself was a prime example. Tartu was to be a conference for those operational key players—themselves split into "delivery partners" and "associates"—to reflect on what it was that they were doing, with the aim being (a) to "capture" the "mutual learning" that had occurred and (b) to work out what it meant to "capture mutual learning" at all. To that end Tricia thought it might be helpful to bring in some outsiders who could "witness and feed back" to the main group. And that was where I would fit in—I was to be part of a group of "critical friends" along with a poet and a videographer. My mission would be to deliver a "global, fresh, insightful, political perspective." When I raised the possibility that I might end up being rather critical of the whole affair, Tricia didn't flinch. "I'm a risk-taker," she said, looking into what from her end of Skype must have looked like my eyes, "and I'm comfortable being a risk-taker. We're in uncharted territory here. The European Union don't know what mobilizing mutual learning is, but they've charged us to do it anyway."

SPEAKING FROM THE global/political perspective, if not necessarily the fresh/insightful one, the last decade or so has seen growing anger at the corruption, incompetence and unaccountability of federal-level bureaucracy: America has the Tea Party, Brazil has its Free Fare Movement, and Europe has groups like the U.K. Independence Party, the French National Front and Alternative for Germany. People are pissed off. This thought was heavy on my mind as I took my fully funded flights from Chicago to Stockholm and then onwards to Tallinn, Estonia's capital, where I strolled around the sun-sharpened Old Town with Tricia and an iPad before a sleepy bus ride brought us to Tartu, a university town known, apparently, as "the Heidelberg of the north," perhaps because of the winding river it bestrides and over which my hotel room was conveniently perched. But by the time I was standing in a circle holding hands with strangers my concern for the taxpayer had begun to fade. I just wanted to know what was happening.

"Welcome to the SiS Family Reunion," Tricia had said as we took our seats in the circle. There were between twenty and thirty members of this family, of varying ages and origins, and I did not feel at home. As we went round the room explaining who we were and what we were doing, it became clear that among our number were not only Europeans—French, German, Austrian, Spanish, English, Polish, Croatian, Estonian—but also three Americans, two Colombians and a Brazilian, all flown in for the occasion. What were they doing here? This was the "Icebreaking Session" for the "Mentoring Associates Networking Day," that much was clear from the program. The difficulty lay in figuring out what a Mentoring Associate was. I couldn't exactly ask at this stage, so I sat back and took notes on my laptop.* Some of the group called themselves "hubs." AB, for example, the friend who had contacted me in the first place, a softly spoken, lightly bearded semi-hippie in his early thirties, explained his role as follows: "I am a hub for four partnerships. My role is to help overcome any obstacles and deal with any blockages. The whole scheme is there to get different projects and cultures to collide because that's when things are created, when two things come together." Chris, meanwhile, a ponytailed forty-something from Vienna, clarified that there were four hubs, and that he was one of them: "Even we hubs don't know what the function of hubs is so we'll have to spend some time to clarify that here."

I should say that by this stage we had achieved a certain level of familiarity and comfort with one another. We began by holding hands and saying our names. Next we played a game where each of us had to walk around the room exchanging names with whoever we bumped into, so that they became us and we became them, until finally we arrived back at our own name. After that came a game where we had to pair off and mime one thing we really liked in primary school and one thing we really disliked. And finally we threw a ball round the room: whoever caught it had to be silent while everyone else said what they knew about that person. This threw up the fact that one of the French contingent, a girl named Vanessa, was the great-granddaughter of a West African royal, or something like that. It also emerged that I was in Tartu as a critical friend with no knowledge of the project, which made it a little less awkward for me to respond to the remarks about hubs by asking what the hell was going on.

The "Mentoring Associates" program turned out to be a fairly intuitive instance of the "mutual learning" concept: each provider of children's university-type activities is paired with a similar organization in a different country; the pair are given €10,000 to visit each other and compare notes; and then at conferences they report back to the rest of the group. There were still some aspects that I didn't understand—each pair apparently participates in a "hub," of which there are four, as well as a "team," of which there are three, and I couldn't get my head around how these overlapping units would actually function—but the basic concept made sense. I did still want to ask why there were non-European partners. The obvious answer was that certain situations in Europe are best

* To the amazement of several ladies over the age of forty, who began by gesturing covertly and eventually came over to confirm with their own eyes, I was touch-typing.

Jules de Balincourt, *Ambitious New Plans*, 2005

understood by comparison with situations outside Europe, but then one of the partnerships appeared to be between Brazil and Kenya. It might have been rude to make such inquiries in the presence of those heavily jetlagged non-Europeans, however, and in any case I felt conscious of dragging everybody down with my non-comprehension, so I let it pass. "It's about me sitting down last night and having the most amazing dinner and talking about what happens when we put Poland and Hawaii together," Tricia concluded.

MUCH OF THE conference was in fact inspirational and/or moving, it has to be said, and by the same token it also has to be said that the parts that were inspirational and/or moving derived disproportionately from SiS Catalyst's man in Hawaii, David Sing, founding executive director of the Nā Pua No'eau Center for Gifted and Talented Native Hawaiian Children. A middle-aged native Hawaiian with black hair, silver goatee and rimless spectacles, Sing is the kind of man who makes you reach for your higher self for fear of letting him down. As a young man he was told he couldn't go to college: "You're not bright, you're lazy and you're poor." He did much more than make it to college: he earned a Ph.D. in education from Claremont Graduate University in California, came back to Hawaii and in 1990 founded the aforementioned Nā Pua No'eau Center, which has become a model for the advancement of indigenous groups worldwide. The stats alone tell quite a story: in 1971 only 4 percent of students enrolled in the National University of Hawaii were native Hawaiians, compared to 22 percent of the population in general; by 2013 that portion had increased sixfold to 24 percent. It's hard to know exactly how much of that is due to Sing and his team, but it's clear they played a large part.

Sing's basic insight, on my understanding, is that for a student to succeed he must want to educate himself, and that in some cases this requires bridging the gap between the educational system and the rest of his life. For many Westerners, there is nothing surprising about studying the canon, sitting in large lecture halls and receiving relatively anonymous feedback. We expect to settle away from our parents; we are used to going unrecognized in daily life; and the canon, whether scientific or humanistic, is in some sense "ours," part of our common inheritance. For a native Hawaiian, however, raised to value his gods and his elders above all, this conception of what it is to be a student may be hard to accept. The canon might appear alien, the campus alienating, a career away from home impious. Sing's idea was to bring the system closer to the student and the student closer to the system. He ran cultural classes for university professors from mainland America to teach them about students' values; he developed a support network for native Hawaiians on campus; he lobbied successfully for general education to include Hawaiian Studies components; he even managed to make native participation part of the mission statement of the University of Hawaii. So much for the supply side. On the demand side, he began a program which encourages teachers to bring out abstract scientific principles through small-group activities that engage students' sense of pride in their heritage and hence elicit their desire to learn: volcanoes are considered local deities in Hawaii, for instance, and a trip to one can occasion geological lessons that in turn fan out into wider scientific questions; something similar goes for examining, building and using canoes like those that brought the first settlers from Polynesia over 1,500 years ago. Small steps these may be, but over 23 years they have led to spectacular results for native Hawaiians, especially as compared to other indigenous groups, and Sing now finds himself in demand from Greenland to Estonia.

In Tartu, Sing seemed like a missionary from another world—a missionary, it might be added, in considerable danger of upsetting the natives. Along with his wife, Nalani, herself a distinguished educator, he frequently took the opportunity to pass on linguistic and cultural tidbits to the group: phrases, practices, pieces of advice. This was all undertaken with the kind of humility and grace that produces intuitive respect on the part of others, but at times it seemed to me that certain members of the SiS Catalyst Family were growing restless. What, after all, did any of this have to do with their own work?

Jerzy Jarosz, Sing's "Mentoring Partner" from the University of Silesia in Poland, was in no doubt. At the "Mentoring Associates Showcase session," he described his initial skepticism when Tricia suggested he go to Hawaii and his surprise at how well it had all worked out. Dressed in black, with an open-necked shirt, designer glasses and suede shoes, his stylishness sitting strangely with the drab college classroom in which we were now crowded, Jarosz gave a clear explanation of what he had learned. Instead of treating subcultures as problematic, he said, Sing had taught him to recognize the specificity of the group and turn it into an advantage, creating a sense of pride and belonging that enables local role models to exert their pull. More generally, Jarosz let it be known, he had fallen in love with Hawaiian culture and values; his bromance with Sing had become a running joke in both their families, and he had several snaps to prove it. The day before, at the "icebreaking" event, Sing had given his version: "Do you know the concept 'blind date?'" he asked, calling to mind a surprisingly illuminating comparison between Tricia and Cilla Black, "Well, we're married now!"

As I mentioned, though, I couldn't help feeling that some among us remained skeptical of the love-in. And at the risk of sounding predictable or prejudiced, I have to report that those who appeared mildly disapproving of such frivolity—on this and other occasions during the conference—were mostly German speakers. I mention this not because I enjoy national stereotypes, although like any Englishman I do,* but because it allows us to see something about SiS Catalyst as a whole, and thereby, perhaps, about the European Union itself.

I HAD COME TO Estonia hoping to find a certain strangeness, perhaps in the form of an administrative subculture where everyone spoke bureaucratese in their sleep—"Deliver the key player to the change agent! Mobilize the mutual learning action plan while there's still time!"—or, more likely, given Tricia's description of SiS Catalyst as a journey through the "uncharted territory" of mutual learning, a conference whose subject was in fact itself: "We have come together on this august occasion to work out what it is that we have come together for." What I found was in some ways stranger. On the surface everything seemed in order: these were serious, intelligent people who had come together with the best of intentions; most of them saw the funny side of the terminology; and the conference sessions were in no way self-swallowing. What was peculiar was just this: every time I asked for a description of SiS Catalyst I seemed to hear something different. Some seemed to think the project was about recruiting the next generation of scientists; others emphasized rectifying social inequalities; but the organizers themselves, the University of Liverpool contingent, kept on talking about training adults to listen to children.

The SiS Catalyst publicity leaflet, for example, is entitled "Children As Change Agents for Science in Society." The front page explains that "SiS Catalyst is based on a very simple idea: that as children are the future, we must involve them in the decisions of today." The inference strikes me as less than obvious—if children are the future, why shouldn't they wait until their time has come?—but in any case, supposing you did want to involve children in the decisions of today, would you really begin with science, as opposed to, say, local politics? And what would it even mean to involve children in decisions concern-

* One of the recurring themes of the conference was the attempt on the part of the English contingent, Tricia at the forefront, to deploy national stereotypes as a means of lightening the mood. "You're late—typical French! Wouldn't get that from the Germans!" This didn't always go down so well.

ing science? The second page of the leaflet only adds to the confusion, since it makes it seem as if science really *isn't* the main point:

> SiS Catalyst is an initiative to foster and support ethical, effective and sustainable engagement between children and the social, cultural, political, scientific and educational institutions which make the decisions that will shape their futures. We believe that enhanced interaction will benefit both children and institutions through exchange of views and improved mutual understanding.

But if science isn't the main point, then why say this project is part of Science in Society? The suggestion is that there is some general project, "Children As Change Agents," of which SiS Catalyst is the science chapter. But there is no such general project. I harp on this because it helps explain a fundamental disconnect at the heart of the conference, one that took me a while to piece together. For of all the people who presented at the conference, and there were many, the only ones to focus on involving children in decision-making were the three keynote speakers.

THE SPEECHES TOOK place in the Assembly Hall of the University of Tartu's "Main Building." Tartu is one of the oldest universities in Eastern Europe, dating back to 1632, and like the rest of Estonia its history is one of domination by Swedes, Germans and Russians. Traveling after the conference, via not only Tallinn but also Toila, Narva and Jõhvi, the last two towns being in fact ethnically Russian, one quickly got the sense of Estonia's flatness and inherent invadability. A single vista frequently combines (i) a couple of austerely elegant buildings of the kind one might expect to find in a Swedish provincial town with (ii) row after row of Soviet-era tower blocks and then (iii) the type of gaudy red-clad prefab shopping center, or rather *box*—complete with supermarket, clothes stores, restaurants and, oddly enough, casino—that seems to have been dropped into Eastern Europe by parachute sometime in the mid-Nineties.* Like Tallinn, though, Tartu has a large and well-enough preserved historic center that the visitor can temporarily forget the horrors of the twentieth century. With

* Western norms of customer service do not seem to have been part of the package, at least if my experience in Narva is any guide. Having installed ourselves in the Central Hotel, conveniently situated between the police station and the strip club, my fellow travelers and I went down and asked the receptionist if she could recommend a place for dinner. "No," she replied.

its six white columns, or "Tuscan pillars," according to the official brochure, the University's Main Building, a neoclassical construction dating back to the Napoleonic Wars, sets the tone. And the Assembly Hall is its crowning jewel, a large ballroom-style affair with 28 white columns supporting a viewing gallery that extends round all four sides. It's the kind of room in which one has visions of Anna Karenina dancing the mazurka; in her stead we had Tricia.

Tricia introduced the session by telling the story of Sebastián, a boy from Medellín, Colombia, who had asked her how he could stop his sister from becoming a prostitute. "I didn't know the answer," Tricia said, audibly welling up, "but I do know that Sebastián believes that he can change the world and I do know that we here in SiS Catalyst can also change the world. So no pressure there then!" At that point the room was rapt, myself included, and that energy carried us through the three talks. Laura Lundy, a professor at Queen's University, Belfast, claimed that children have a human right to participate in decisions that affect them. Zack Kopplin, a fresh-faced freshman at Rice University, explained how as a high-school student he had created a campaign against the teaching of creationism. Margit Sutrop, head of the University of Tartu's Center for Ethics, argued that teachers ought to be shaping students into citizens who are willing and able to reflect on their own values. The talks were provocative and engaging, and much could be said about each of them. But they were all of a piece with Tricia's opening in one important sense: they had very little to do with the European Union's Science in Society agenda. Sutrop was advocating the creation of philosophically minded citizens and Kopplin was complaining about American backwardness. Lundy did touch on research into ways of discovering children's preferences concerning science classes, but she spent most of her time arguing that such preference-pumping was a human right.* Those looking for help on

* Unlike most of the audience, I found this unconvincing. Human rights are, as Lundy began by saying, the rights we have simply in virtue of being human beings. The question from a philosophical standpoint is whether we should think that that set has any members, and if so how many. Human rights law is an artifact of international treaties rather than philosophical reasoning, and the two can come apart fairly quickly. The 1948 Universal Declaration of Human Rights, for example, famously includes the right to a paid vacation (Article 24), which is clearly *not* something that we are entitled to simply in virtue of being human, or else nomadic life would be a humanitarian scandal. (I should say that the 1948 Declaration is not itself a legally binding treaty, but it nevertheless exemplifies the problems found in schedules of rights that *are* legally binding.) Lundy's subject was the 1989 UN Convention on the Rights of the Child, which seems to suffer from exactly the same problem. Article 29, for instance, commits signatory governments to direct education towards, among other things, "the development of respect for the natural environment." It would be hard to argue with a straight face that simply in virtue of being a human being one has the right to be educated into environmentalism; and as soon as we go for a looser interpretation of the word "respect," the so-called right is emptied of all meaning. So we cannot assume that just because something is called a "human right" in an international treaty it really *is* a human right,

their "children's university" projects could have been forgiven for thinking they were at the wrong conference. On the plus side, they were in the majority.

But even among those whose interests lay less in "listening to children" than in educating them—and yes, I recognize that the two ought to be related—there seemed to exist a significant division over priorities. My default move during the conference's quiet moments was to go around telling people I didn't understand what exactly the conference was about and asking if they could give me a unifying principle. Aside from the learning-from-children angle, which was stressed mostly by the leadership and even then not consistently, most participants emphasized both science education and social mobility. But while some seemed to think science education important insofar as it might hold the key to increased social mobility, others seemed to find social mobility important insofar as it might hold the key to scientific progress. It's not hard to see how both groups could profit from working together. But if resources are tight, as they usually are, and decisions need to be made, as they always do, at some point you would imagine that one of these priorities will have to win out. If the goal is to recruit new scientists, the emphasis should be on scouring every nook and cranny to find talent; if the goal is to promote equality, it should be on encouraging kids of all ability levels.

And this brings us back to the German speakers. Tricia had told me in our original Skype call that SiS Catalyst was a sort of hybrid between the Vienna-led European Children's University Network (EUCU.NET) and the European Access Network (EAN), based at the University of Roehampton in the U.K. Following in the footsteps of the University of Tübingen in Germany, which created the first "children's university"—i.e. open-day/festival program—in 2002, the Viennese had successfully developed a network of such schemes funded by the European Union. Tricia's objection was that these schemes, however innovative, were mostly for children with ambitious and motivated parents rather than the poor or excluded.* She had therefore had the idea of applying for European funding to harness the same models for the benefit of what she called "locally defined minorities." In other words, her plan was to make science education serve social mobility. Now on the face of it this agenda has little to do with "The

---

something that as moral agents we are unconditionally committed to respecting. Granted, when the treaty has become law in a signatory country it becomes a "positive" (or actually existing) right along with all the other rights provided by national law. In this way the "human right" can become a resource that campaigners can draw upon in litigation and so on. But campaigners should not confuse themselves into thinking that anything more than that is going on—for national laws, as we all know, can be both just and unjust.

* For example, the Viennese project apparently reached children not through their schools but through ads placed in newspapers, a strategy presupposing a high degree of parental involvement.

Potential and Ethics of Learning from Children," to use the official title of the Tartu conference. But to see the connection, as I did only months later, is to appreciate Tricia's entrepreneurial genius.

MY DISSERTATION WAS in large part about the ideal of "functional" institutions: in an ideal society, I claim, the various parts of each institution would fit together harmoniously, such that each part plays a particular role in bringing about the good at which the institution as a whole aims, with that institution in turn being one part of a larger harmonious whole. This is a simple enough idea, and in some sense it is really quite trivial, even if I do draw it out of Plato. What makes it less trivial, in my view, is simply that so few institutions actually are coherent in this way, whether on the micro or the macro level. The way I express that is to say that most are to some degree either "non-functional" or "dysfunctional"—they are either incoherent, lacking a common thread that would unify them, or organized but with respect to the wrong goal. You might think of the former by analogy to a playground soccer team where everyone chases the ball rather than staying in defined positions, such that the players are not playing *as a team*, and the latter along the lines of the common protest that capitalist news organizations ultimately privilege shareholder value over informing the public. This is why I pricked up my ears when Tricia first told me that one of the goals of the mobilizing mutual learning action plan was to work out what mutual learning actually was. It was amusing, but it also seemed to challenge the idea that institutions *should* be functional. It therefore inflamed in me an insecurity that may be common to all academic pontificators—an anxiety that the "real world," a world from which we feel necessarily and irreparably cut off, might turn out to contain more things than are dreamt of in our philosophy.

The SiS Catalyst grant application does at first seem to reject the functional ideal. A section entitled "Progress Beyond The State of the Art" gives the following account of the "SiS Catalyst Learning Process":

> SiS Catalyst not only promotes so called "Single Loop Learning" (present when goals, values, frameworks and strategies are taken for granted and directed toward making the strategy more effective), but also "Double-loop learning" (involves questioning the role of the framing and learning systems which underlie actual goals and strategies) and "Meta-Learning," which means inquiring the process of learning and thinking about ways to improve discussion about values underlying strategies. ... All Work Pack-

> ages ... are embedded within the SiS-Catalyst learning cycle and deliver instruments and mechanisms to promote the different levels of learning.*

This is all rather philosophical, even Socratic. Rather than merely asking the practical question of how we can go about φ-ing, it suggests, we should raise the question of why we want to φ in the first place, and then the question of what it would be to answer that question well, and so on, presumably, ad infinitum. In some sense, then, it really is true that the learning SiS Catalyst hopes to achieve is learning about itself. But this is not necessarily opposed to the functional ideal—it may in fact presume it, since it would make no sense to engage in second- and third-order reflection unless one were ultimately trying to get clear on one's first-order goals. And in any case the process must start with a provisional definition of goals in order for the "loops" to get started. So even for an organization as committed to the reflexive learning process as SiS Catalyst, we are still entitled to expect a certain amount of functional thinking from the start.

Section B1.2.1 of the grant application, "The Overall Objectives of the Project," claims there are three goals: (1) to capture mutual learning concerning "how to include children in the dialogue between society and the scientific and technological community"; (2) to build models of how to do this that can then be "rolled out in order to build the capacity of new-comers"; and (3) "to build tools which enable Higher Education Institutions to self-evaluate and test their progress of enriching their aspirations of Lifelong Learning and social inclusion with SiS activities ... and to contextual these in regional, national, European and global contexts." Aside from the bizarre prose—one's horror is doubled when one "contextuals" all this in the education context—this list is a conceptual mystery. First of all, (2) looks like a means of achieving (1) rather than an objective per se, unless the emphasis is firmly placed on the goal of "rolling out," which it is not. And where did (3) come from? No mention was made in (1) and (2) of lifelong learning and social inclusion as being goals, so why are we now working out how to measure them? And this, it should be stressed, is the inconsistency just within Section B1.2.1. Elsewhere in the prospectus we hear that the project will focus on children aged 8-14 because "inequalities in the achievement of children from low and high income backgrounds emerge extremely early, well before schooling begins." Given that logic, shouldn't we be focusing on pre-

* These ideas are credited to the organizational theorists Chris Argyris and Donald Schön; the grammar is all SiS Catalyst.

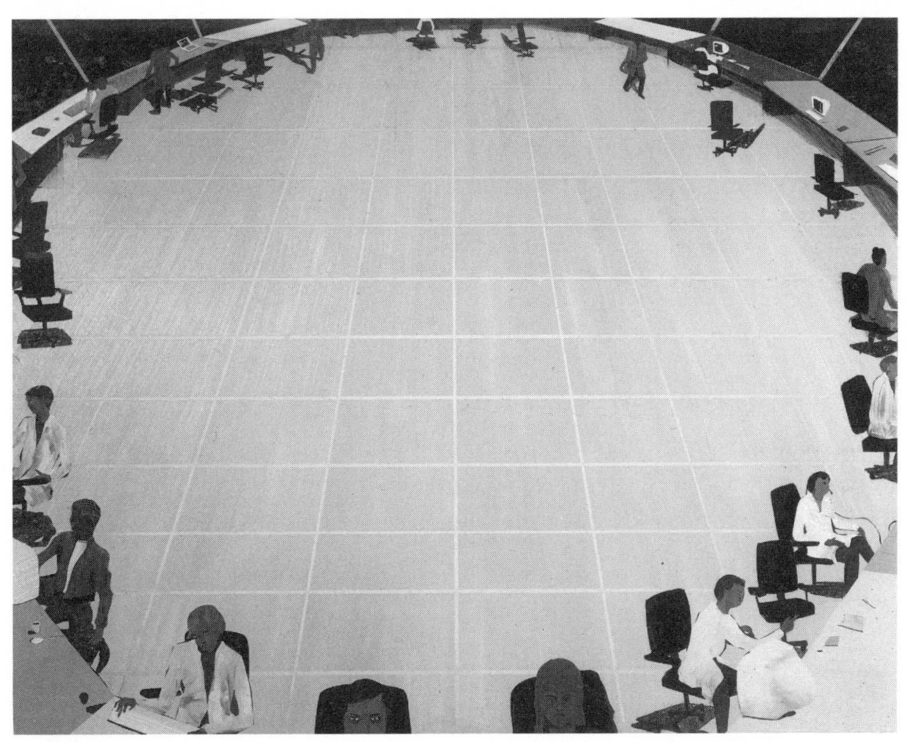

Jules de Balincourt, *The Watchtower*, 2005

school children? And if rectifying inequality is the guiding ambition, why isn't it mentioned in B1.2.1?

There is no need to go deeper into this document. Suffice it to say that to the degree that conference participants seemed unsure of what was tying the whole thing together, they were onto something.* And I suspect this is what the German speakers were objecting to, however implicitly. Whether because of ingrained cultural factors of the sort that an Englishman like myself would never dream of bringing up, or because of the Viennese experience in running a closely related European project in somewhat different fashion, they seemed skeptical of an institution without a well-defined function.† I was on their side back in Tartu. Now I'm not so sure.

"ARGUMENTATIVE INCOMPLETE CONFUSING unclear complex challenging difficult isolating technical exhausting categorized repetitive fractured unwieldy." We were in the conference's final session, the meeting of the Scientific Advisory Board, and the learning process was coming to a boil under the benign eye of one Bastian Baumann, higher-education consultant and "external evaluator" for SiS Catalyst. A tall and calming man whose website advertises him as "very active in the area of Quality Assurance"—so active, in fact, that he has even served to assure the quality of several quality assurance agencies, not to mention the European Association of Quality Assurance Agencies (ENQA)—Bastian had divided us into three groups, Tricia not included, and instructed us to reflect on the strengths and weaknesses of the SiS Catalyst project. How would we explain them to our next-door neighbor, assuming we were on speaking terms? Which adjectives would we use? We had split off and written down ideas and now we were back together to hear the results. It was a little awk-

* AB did tell me that he had never worked with anyone so impressive as his new-ish colleague Blaise, a somewhat debonair Frenchman who seemed to serve as something like Tricia's personal assistant (i.e. boss) throughout the conference—for unlike everyone else, Blaise had been able to grasp the structure of the project immediately. I confess this made me a little suspicious of Blaise.

† It's difficult to provide hard evidence to back up this feeling, so it may just be a projection on my part. I do remember that during the bonhomie of the "SiS Family Reunion," Chris from Vienna mentioned that even though it was boring when compared to cultural exchange and so on, budgeting was the most important thing for mentoring partners to learn from one another. It was little incidents like this that gave me my impression, I think—just a general sense that if the Viennese were in charge things would be running differently.

ward to have all those negative adjectives stacked up there in front of everyone, not least because Tricia's right eye was shot with blood that day like the weeping Madonna of Civitavecchia. But it also felt healthy to have the complaints out in the open. And anyway the positives had come first: "Engaging diverse visionary flexible speedy exciting expert strong thought-provoking sharing reflective inspiring comforting unique sympathetic fun reflexive dynamic ambitious changing grateful mission-led international interesting innovative creative powerful shiny."

We then went into the second phase, described by Bastian as a modified version of the "World Café," a Californian management technique in which group discussions take place at different tables, with a "host" at each taking notes; the "guests" then switch tables and their new host brings them up to speed on his table's previous discussion before soliciting new thoughts; and finally each host presents his table's findings to the whole group. The World Café is "a powerful social technology," its promotional materials claim, but also "a way of thinking and being together sourced in a philosophy of conversational leadership." To translate back into terms that will no doubt be more familiar and more natural to the reader by now: what the World Café offers is, in short, in brief, in sum, a *mobilizing mutual learning action plan.*

And it worked. We had three tables organized around three different themes: Impact; Sustainability; and Group Dynamics. In a bizarre twist, the host of the Group Dynamics table turned out to be me. This meant that it was I that produced the penultimate action of the conference, presenting a report concerning what *we* could do to improve *our* organization, all the while (a) knowing very little about the organization or the situation—I would only read the founding documents on my return, and at this stage I still hadn't put my finger on the three different goals—and (b) nursing a hangover from a student bar up a narrow staircase where the floors were crooked and the walls were orange and an army recruit was on his last night out and the shots came in units of ten.

My table had come up with two big suggestions. One was to create a visualization of the structure of SiS Catalyst as a whole. It would be a simple map that would allow members to see whose work they were drawing on and whose work they were feeding into, creating a sense of membership and purpose. "If the division of labor is too complex," I said, casting matters into my own mold like a good academic, "it can cause problems. You think, 'I have my project and that's what I care about.' There might be a territorialism caused by not being able to see how one's work fits into a larger whole."

Our other suggestion concerned jargon. "I'm just a bit confused about the terminology," someone had said earlier in the day. "Is what is now called 'the policy seminar' equivalent to what was previously called 'national capacity-building intervention'?" Our idea was to create a wiki-glossary where terms and policies and units would be defined by the group as a collective. "Why is it that we can't talk about things with normal terms that actually have a referent?" I asked, a little over-aggressively. "A term like 'Work Package 6,' in principle that could mean anything, whereas 'listening to children' is a bit more informative. I suspect that if we did a test right now and we got each of us to write down the meaning of each work package we wouldn't get 100 percent correct answers—there would be some red ink."

Bastian and I had spoken during the coffee break that followed the previous day's session on "Orientation and Requirements of the SiS Catalyst Badges Ecosystem." I asked him what his role as external evaluator entailed. He said he was partly there to help shape the project by giving feedback on methodology, but that his main task was to give a final report on the project's performance to Tricia: this would then be one of the "deliverables" that SiS Catalyst would send to Brussels at the end of the project. "And who is it in Brussels that it gets sent to when it gets sent to Brussels?" I asked, my mind turning to the pipes and pulleys of Terry Gilliam's *Brazil*. "Within the Directorate-General for Education, Audiovisual Services and Culture," Bastian replied, "they have a specific agency to deal with Framework Seven projects. It's a horrible building. I've been there a couple of times and you're usually locked away in a cellar without any windows and you have to evaluate certain things."*

He was happier in Tartu. After my presentation he tended to us as a preacher to his flock. "I have one question: How many of you have participated in Framework-funded projects before?" A couple of hands. "That becomes quite evident for two reasons. One is that people tend to get a bit unhappy with how things are going in a project. But there is no perfect project. It just doesn't exist. There are always shortcomings, always flaws. What I think when I compare this project with others is that yes, it is very ambitious, but it is also dynamic and there is so much commitment and enthusiasm from the vast majority of people that there is a lot of work that gets done between meetings. Therefore the word I would like to use to describe the project is 'hungry.' People are hungry to achieve results, to make an impact, and that is a very positive feature. When a university has been running the same project for the last 25 years with the same people, people are not hungry any more, they just see it as a means of funding a

---

* Bastian may have misspoken regarding the institutional structure. According to Wikipedia there are two different units, first the Directorate-General for Education and Culture, and then the Education, Audiovisual and Culture Executive Agency, which the Directorate-General oversees. Presumably the specific agency that Bastian referred to is located within the Education, Audiovisual and Culture Executive Agency.

position." And with that we were sent on our way. The fourth conference of the SiS Catalyst odyssey had come to an end.

BACK IN CHICAGO I began trying to piece things together. I went over my notes and recordings. I subjected the official leaflets and 130-page funding bid to a close reading. But at a certain point I concluded that I would never be able to make sense of SiS Catalyst without understanding the whole of which it is a part.

The SiS of SiS Catalyst stands for "Science in Society," one of many funding priorities incorporated in the European Union's seven-year, €50 billion science budget, the "Seventh Framework Programme for Research and Technological Development," known to its friends as "FP7." FP7, which runs from 2007 to 2014, has two overarching goals, according to the "pocket guide for newcomers": to strengthen the scientific and technological base of European industry; and to increase its international competitiveness while promoting research that supports other E.U. policies. These goals will be achieved via five "building blocks", each with its own budget allocation: "Cooperation," "Ideas," "People," "Capacities" and, in the kind of spectacular but completely unheralded category shift that provides a perpetual source of pleasure to readers of E.U. documents, "Nuclear Research." "Science in Society" fits in as part of the Capacities block, whose guiding ambition is "[to strengthen] the research capacities that Europe needs if it is to become a thriving knowledge-based economy."

What exactly "Science in Society" means turns out to be somewhat hard to say. "The defining characteristic of Euro English is that nobody knows what it means," a friend who deals with the E.U. in her capacity as a policy analyst wrote to me when I pled for help. "You may be interested to know that this has itself been the topic of E.U. deliberation," she went on, pointing me to an official document entitled "A Brief List of Misused English Terms in E.U. publications"—which brief list runs, I should say, to 58 pages.* But jargon is a

* *Example*: "[The European Parliament] ... calls for it to be made possible for the actors involved in the management of operational programmes to influence conditionalities." *Admonishment:* "'Conditionality' is a clumsy word that should be used parsimoniously (see 'Reasonability'). Moreover, it is not an erudite synonym of 'condition' but a derivative of 'conditional' and means simply 'the state of being conditional.' Finally, it is an uncountable noun (see introduction) that cannot be used in the plural, despite the 156 plural hits in EUR-Lex. It should perhaps be noted that this word is also used, equally incomprehensibly, by the IMF." *Suggested Alternative*: "Often just 'conditions' or 'the conditions imposed/set'."

symptom, not a cause. Anthropologists have noted that jargon functions like a shibboleth, a way of excluding outsiders. George Orwell stressed that it can be used to cover up unpleasant facts. It also just permits one to avoid the time-consuming and often unpleasant business of nailing down concepts. And this conceptual permissiveness transcends jargon per se.

The "Science in Society" website begins with some ruminations on the value of science ("Although we rarely think about it, science makes extraordinary things possible. At the flick of a switch, we have light and electricity. When we are ill, science helps us get better") before declaring that "scientific endeavor is as much about us as it is for us. Its place in society, therefore, is not to unfold quietly at the sidelines but to become a fundamental part of the game. Now more than ever, science must engage with us, and we must engage with science." This sounds vague, wrong and quite possibly nonsensical, but what follows is comparatively concrete.

The first goal of Science in Society is to "build gateways with the public," creating opportunities "for scientists and the general public to exchange views in a two-way dialogue of mutual respect and trust."* The second goal is to "inspire the next era of scientists," encouraging young people, especially women, to consider careers in science. And the plan is then to "integrate science into the mix" by commissioning scientific research into how best to achieve these goals. To summarize, then, according to the homepage the basic idea of Science in Society

* It's hard to know what to make of this at first—one can't envisage much dialogue between the general public and physicists looking for dark matter—but it turns out that the discussions are supposed to be over ethical and political questions, which are by their nature non-scientific. It remains unclear how this dialogue is supposed to take place. Sometimes it seems the E.U. has "Civil Society Organisations" (CSOs) in mind when it says "the general public," as if there were a neat chain whereby ordinary citizens find their views reflected by non-profit advocacy groups and then those groups communicate with scientists who adjust their research priorities accordingly. Where this idea comes from, or why it should trump the democratic process at the national level, is unclear, but the concrete result is the creation of a new "funding scheme" called "Research for the Benefit of Specific Groups—Civil Society Organisations," which allows CSOs to commission "Research Organisations" (universities?) to conduct research on their behalf using European funding. At other times the picture seems totally different: at one point, for instance, we hear that a model of "real engagement and two-way dialogue between researchers and the public" was the "Meeting of Minds (European Citizens' Deliberation on Brain Science)," a 2005-6 exercise in which 126 citizens were chosen at random to discuss questions surrounding the regulation of brain science. The ensuing report is somewhat thrilling for anyone who has wondered what deliberative democracy might look like, but I haven't been able to investigate (a) whether any of its recommendations were ever acted upon; (b) whether the experiment has been repeated; or (c) how much the whole thing cost. It has to be noted, perhaps particularly with respect to (c), that the 126 citizens were not left to produce their report unaided: they seem to have been accompanied in their efforts by no less than 139 "resource persons" (experts) as well as a team of 22 facilitators, writers and editors.

is to make the institutions of European science more accessible to European citizens. So far, so good.

But then the schizophrenia/mendacity sets in. For on a subsequent page ("Science in Society in FP7") we read that "the overarching objective of the Programme is to make the SiS perspective a core element of E.U. research policy, helping shape its future priorities and ways of operating." And what that means, when you think about it, is that the guiding ambition of the project is in fact its own perpetuation.

Just a mistake? Maybe. But this kind of ambiguity turns up at the micro level as well. Science in Society is itself divided into five subsections, including "Mobilising Mutual Learning Action Plans" (MMLs), under which SiS Catalyst falls.* The other subsections are "Policy Initiatives"; "Ethics Review"; "Scientific Information and Expertise for Policy Support in Europe" (SINAPSE); and "Monitoring Activities of Science in Society in Europe" (MASIS). This last is initially described as an attempt to work out ("monitor") what the role of science in European society currently is, or, to allow the author's voice free rein, "what are cutting edge issues and what are challenging futures." So far, so good—again. On another page, however, we hear that MASIS "aims to increase the visibility of SiS activities, and therefore their impact on European policymaking and society at large." So monitoring has become acting, acting has become advertising, and such advertising has found its primary target in Brussels.

Here is my hypothesis. Each European unit has two goals, one external and one internal. The external goal is specific: it is that for the sake of which the unit was initially funded. The internal goal is generic: it consists in the unit's self-perpetuation via the next round of funding, which will be the Eighth Framework of 2014—or at least it would be, had the E.U. not renamed it "Horizon 2020," the replacement of "Framework" by "Horizon" seemingly designed with the express intention of making things just that little bit less clear for ordinary people.

If this hypothesis is correct then the internal goal of Science in Society is not in itself remarkable. The external one, on the other hand, is worth pondering. Science in Society aims (1) to encourage dialogue between scientists and the general public and (2) to shepherd young people into scientific careers. Given

* The reader may not be surprised to learn that it turns out to be more than a little difficult to pin down exactly what a mobilizing mutual learning action plan is—Hegel will seem like a doddle after this—but my sense from the various websites is that each year different goals (or "thematics") are designated from on high, and that instead of trying to actually achieve (or "deliver") one of these goals, applicants for MML funding should focus on ensuring that groups already working towards the goal, both inside and outside academia, are sharing information and experiences.

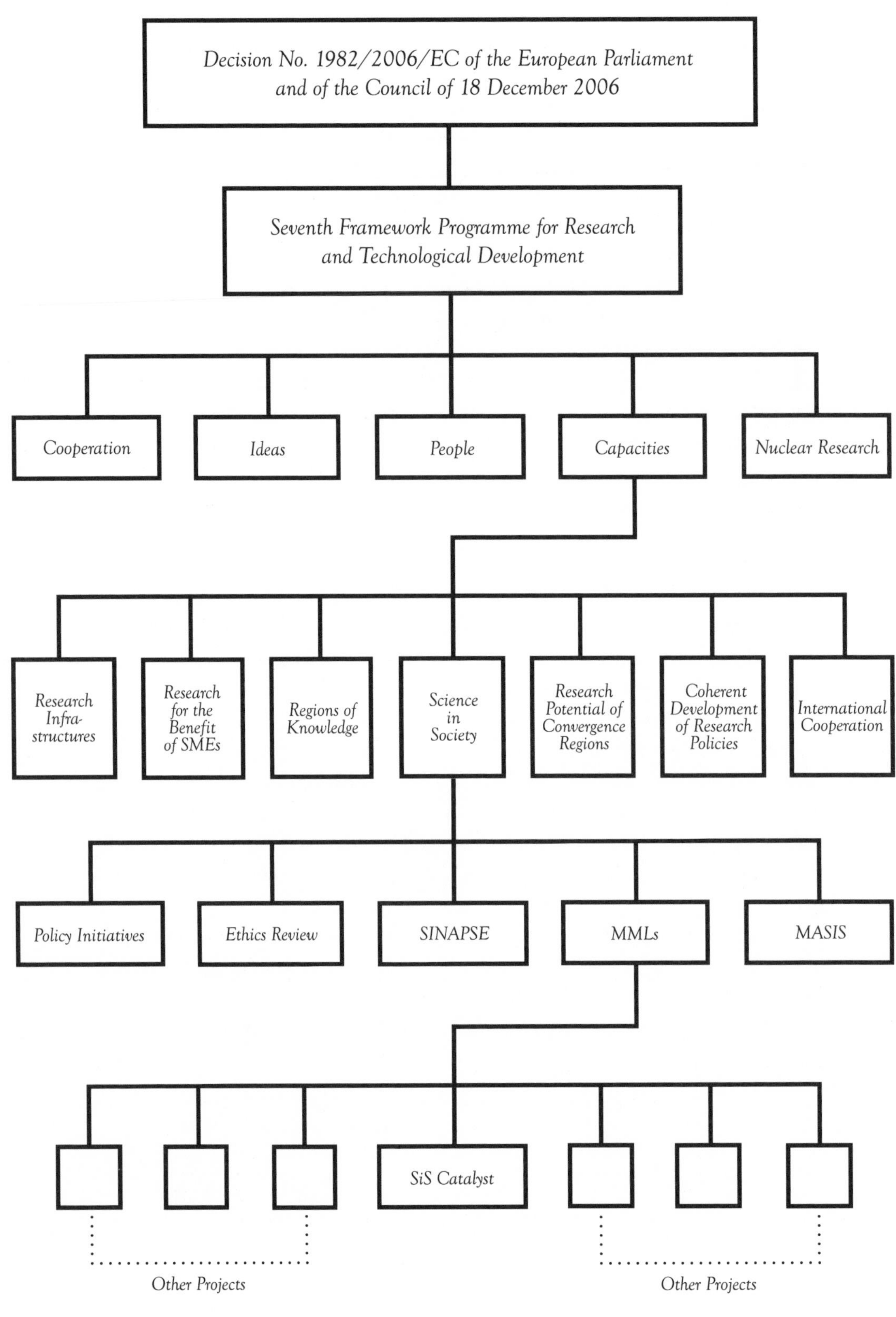

Decision No. 1982/2006/EC of the European Parliament and of the Council of 18 December 2006
Seventh Framework Programme for Research and Technological Development
Cooperation
Ideas
People
Capacities
Nuclear Research
Research Infra-structures
Research for the Benefit of SMEs
Regions of Knowledge
Science in Society
Research Potential of Convergence Regions
Coherent Development of Research Policies
International Cooperation
Policy Initiatives
Ethics Review
SINAPSE
MMLs
MASIS
SiS Catalyst
Other Projects
Other Projects

that Science in Society forms part of the Capacities section of FP7, we can infer that the reason why (1) and (2) are considered valuable is that they will help to build up "the research capacities that Europe needs if it is to become a thriving knowledge-based economy." And the reason why *that* would be valuable, as with FP7 as a whole, is that it will increase European competitiveness relative to other economies.

TRICIA DID TELL me that she had never directed a project of this size before, despite her many years of receiving European funding, and that it had been a struggle. You're responding to an opaque set of criteria, including in this case the nebulous idea of mobilizing mutual learning, and you're just trying to make things sound right. "I was the primary writer of the work description [i.e. the plan] and I don't think I recognized what it was for about eighteen months. I remember going to this invited workshop from the European Commission on Mobilizing Mutual Learning Action Plans and I remember thinking, 'Oh yes, that's what we are!'" So the non-functionality of SiS Catalyst as an organization may have been partly caused by simple inexperience on her part.

But a more important factor may have been her idealism. Idealism is a laudable quality, but it brings with it one big danger: wishful thinking. And wishful thinking stalks SiS Catalyst. My presence at the Tartu conference was itself evidence of that. Tricia's last-minute attempt to recruit a video artist and a performance artist from Sweden having failed, my only colleague in the "critical friends" brigade was Joonas, an Estonian caricaturist who actually looked like a caricature, oddly enough, being wiry and angular, blond to the point of extinction and equipped with an Adam's apple so pronounced he resembled a stork. (Joonas refused my repeated invitations to see the funny side of the conference, but I didn't take it personally: he seemed to have taken a vow of silence.) Our mission was partly to contribute some reflections from the outside, but mostly to help spread the word about SiS Catalyst. And what was the target, exactly? Well, Tricia explained as we meandered through the windy cobbled streets and steep steps of old Tallinn, "Unless the learning is shared with ten million hits, it's not global." Ten *million* hits? The conversation then continued:

> The thing is, the good stuff is there. You look at United Nations stuff, it's good, you look at the Council of Europe, it's good stuff, you look at the American Declaration of Independence, it's good stuff—but how is

> that good stuff actually implemented? We don't need to reinvent the good stuff, we just need to recognize the good stuff and then move on. That's where I think we are at the University of Tartu, to get to the next stage, which is from collective understanding to how an individual can make a difference. And I'm going to start the conference with a young man, Sebastián, that I met in Colombia, who is 17, his father was murdered when he was a child, he's had a really tough life, and he says, "I know I can change the world. I know that the things I do can change the world." And that's not religious fanaticism, that's just ownership of the change, because of course we all change the world with everything we do. We're just very easily distracted!

Now Tricia is clearly an outlier in the SiS Catalyst family, but this last move was made by many others at the conference: you begin with a description that marks someone out as particularly valuable, like "key player" or "change agent," and then you extend it to every child, or everybody in the room, or just every human being in general. This empties the term of all meaning, of course, but as a psychological process it's amazing to observe—it's wishful thinking *in action*, as it were. And this helps explain what's going on with SiS Catalyst's institutional structure.*

There are, as I have been stressing, three very different goals at the heart of SiS Catalyst: learning from children; fighting inequality; and promoting scientific careers. But whereas I see non-function, parts pulling away from each other, I suspect that Tricia and her University of Liverpool team would see an ideal blend. After all, if the best way to combat inequality happens to be to get youngsters from poor backgrounds into science, and the best way to get them

---

* Another example is SiS Catalyst's definition of science so as to include the humanities: "In this project, 'science' refers to the full range of academic disciplines. This includes the natural and physical sciences, the applied sciences, mathematics, nanotechnology and genomics, newly emerging and interdisciplinary fields as well as to the social sciences and humanities, which are critical to the interface between science and society." This doesn't come from nowhere: the German language pictures the humanities as knowledge-producing *Wissenschaften* just like the natural and social sciences, only with a different object, namely culture (*Geist*). Personally I think of this as the misleading vestige of the German nineteenth century, in which philology was understood as the paradigm instance of a humanistic discipline, and hence the humanities were viewed as regularly and reliably productive of knowledge, i.e. *wissenschaftlich*. I don't think this model fits, say, literary criticism. But even if it does fit, it remains hard to see how work in the humanities would increase economic competitiveness. So calling the humanities part of science doesn't actually solve the problem of their marginalization under the European Union's funding frameworks. It just allows one to pretend the problem does not exist.

into science happens to be to allow them to shape their own learning processes, what's not to like? This is why the Hawaiian experience looms so large for SiS Catalyst: it's the perfect example of how the three priorities can be reconciled to immense practical effect. But the idea that things will always work so neatly is simply wishful thinking. The notion that children between the ages of 8 and 14 have any kind of wisdom about what it would be good for them to learn strikes me as deeply questionable; indeed, it strikes me as questionable whether even college-age kids have this kind of wisdom. (The Hawaiian example of "listening to children," which is supposed to provide universal lessons, is in fact rather particular in the sense that it revolves around the fact of overcoming *cultural* differences between children and their educators, rather than *generational* ones.) In any case, a more mobile society is not necessarily a more equal one: there will be winners and losers in this educational race, just like in any other, and the question will be how we as a society distribute rewards between winners and losers. If we really want a more equal society, what we need is not science but philosophy and economics.*

When you start looking at it like that, though, you begin to appreciate what a wonder Tricia had performed. There was a reason why she had responded to my initial question as to the purpose of SiS Catalyst by referring to the difficulty of securing funding. For the stark fact is that Science in Society, the E.U. project under which SiS Catalyst falls, has *nothing at all to do with equality*. Its goal is to foster a set of capacities in the European population such that Europe becomes more competitive on the international marketplace. Gender equality does come up in the context of ways of recruiting more scientists, but not because of any considerations having to do with justice per se. Social equality might in principle do likewise, but (a) it doesn't and (b) even if did, it would still be equality for the sake of recruitment for the sake of technological development for the sake of economic competitiveness, which amounts to the kind of "meritocratic" vision of equality that even Margaret Thatcher would have endorsed. It's a pretty small-minded vision of science and it's a pretty small-minded vision of society. I would even call it cynical, were it not for my suspicion that it's no one's idea of the good, but rather traces back to the fact that the European Union is itself a non-functional institution that has never resolved the basic question of what

* One might wonder, for instance, whether there isn't simply an arms race of qualifications underway, such that to the degree that more working-class students get B.A.s, more middle-class students will seek M.A.s to distinguish themselves, and so on ad infinitum, in which case by focusing on disparities in higher education we would risk of mistaking an effect for a cause.

it exists for. In such a context, the lowest common denominator tends to win out—and the lowest common denominator tends to be money.

In short, then, what the European Union wants from Science in Society is dysfunctional: functional institutions organized around an end that is itself distorted, whether due to a mistaken understanding of the good in question (maybe someone somewhere really does believe that education is only valuable for economic reasons) or because the nexus in which it sits (the European Union) is itself incoherent or non-functional. And what Tricia managed to do, by means of a certain amount of vagueness and obfuscation in the grant application, was to escape this vision—to use confusion over what exactly mutual learning means, and how that relates to children and to competitiveness, to smuggle in equality as a self-standing goal for SiS Catalyst. However much the project is willing to pay lip service to the idea of raising European competitiveness—"SiS Catalyst makes a contribution towards raising the culture of innovation throughout the society as a whole"—nothing could be further from the spirit of the conference that I witnessed, which, I should probably mention, had a whole talk devoted to Peruvian ballet dancers. Which isn't to say that I fully understand that spirit, of course, or that it was completely coherent. But it does seem to me that Tricia had pulled something off. She had managed to use non-function to combat dysfunction. I don't know how conscious this was, or how complete, but it strikes me as worthy of note; it's a possibility I had theretofore ignored in my own conceptualization of institutions. More importantly, it also strikes me as noble in a way that only idealism can be. Yes, idealism can lead to wishful thinking—but it is precisely their refusal to accept reality that permits idealists to reshape the world. In her final project before retirement, Tricia, a woman who had spent her whole career working to help disadvantaged kids up the ladder, refused to give in to the logic of the Seventh Framework Programme for Research and Technological Development. When she called herself a risk-taker in our original Skype conversation I thought of David Brent. But it was true. She *was* a risk-taker. And it may well be that some kids, somewhere, are the better for it.

ON THE EVE of the next SiS Catalyst conference, which took place in Lodz, Poland, and having missed by a few days the deadline agreed upon in advance with AB, I delivered this essay, or a version thereof, to Tricia. I waited. And then came the response. "Delicious rumblings and repercussions around your essay," Tricia wrote. It had been received well for the most part, she said, even if it contained a few factual errors:

> Chris from KUW—40 something with a pony tail—quoted the essay in our final plenary as he described—coming at it with real clarity—the three conflicting aspects of SiS Catalyst—or the three sides of a pyramid shaped mountain—as I had translated them. It was wonderful—because we could all see—probably for the first time—that we are operating on a three sided mountain, we could see which mountain face was our personal priority/passion—but also see that some people prioritized different sides but collectively we were trying to climb all three sides at once. Great stuff!

So taken was Tricia with the essay, in fact, that she wanted to count it as an "external evaluation" such that it would "form part of our final report to the European Commission at the end of 2014 within Work Package 3." What I had managed to produce, in other words, was a *deliverable.**

Unlike Joonas, then, who apparently disappeared without producing a single cartoon—perhaps he was actually the performance artist from Sweden—at least I hadn't let Tricia down. That motivation loomed largely as I wrote the essay, I confess. I was invited to the conference as an outside evaluator, or "rapporteur," and given that I knew nothing whatsoever of the subject matter, the temptation was to treat it as something of a lark, to look for the comedy and only the comedy. There *was* comedy, for sure. But however much of a mess the European Union and its projects are, however much one wants to sneer, to spend a week with men and women dedicated to improving the lot of the poorest is to feel oneself called to earnestness and to admiration. The experience of sitting at dinner with David Sing in a concrete hexagon above the Emajõgi river and feeling myself morally small, humbled, as I looked into the kindness of his eyes, was in fact one that I had repeatedly throughout the week—as I listened, to give just one example, to the story of Karim, an 18-year-old French boy with a host of brothers and sisters to look after, who somehow found the motivation and the energy to organize a three-day conference on physics thanks to the encouragement of an SiS Catalyst partner organization named Paris-Montagne. Employed as a critic, my job was of course to criticize. But idealists are captivating—you don't want to let them down. Did that corrupt my judgment? Did I find a silver

* It later materialized that some of Tricia's colleagues—which ones you can probably guess—objected to the use of my essay as a deliverable, so I don't know what will happen in the end.

lining because I went looking for one? I don't know. I don't think so. But at any rate it was an odd position to be in and I'm not sure I would want to repeat it. As I say that, though, I glance back at the close of Tricia's email:

> Anyway currently planning to get a group of German speaking children onto a reservation in Montana for week next July to work with a group of Native Americans to make a video of their Recommendations for the future, alongside a couple of student interns, including one from a Roma community who will be looking at the Medicine Wheel based curriculum and it's applicability within Europe—so if you want to write another essay—just let me know!

And I feel a little twitch.

symposium

what is science for?

WHAT IS SCIENCE FOR?

A PORTFOLIO

by D. Graham Burnett *and* Mark Dion

Collecting Cabinet, 1993
All images courtesy of Mark Dion and Tanya Bonakdar Gallery

IN THIS PORTFOLIO of curated texts and visual material, D. Graham Burnett and Mark Dion—who shared a studio for a year while each working at the intersection of artistic practice and the history of science—juxtapose a collection of telling historical quotations with images that evoke collective fantasies of rational inquiry into nature. The result explores the rhetorical dimensions of both representing science and opining as to its purpose.

Trichechus manatus latirostris, 2013

"After all, what is science for, if it be not to bring man and nature to embrace each other rapturously, lovingly, responsively?"

HILDERIC FRIEND, "NEW WORLD NATURE-LOVERS," *HARDWICKE'S SCIENCE-GOSSIP*, 1891

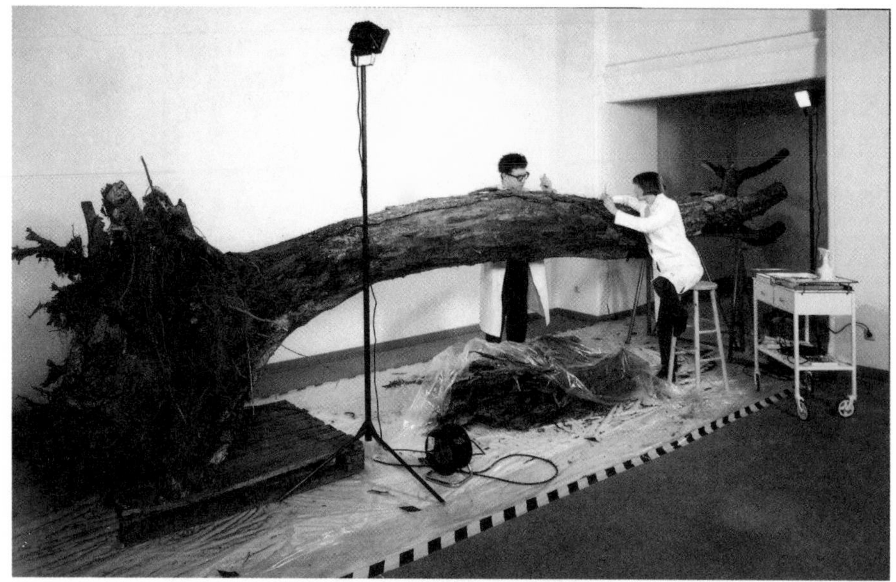

The Great Munich Bug Hunt, 1993

"Pestilence follows dirt; health, cleanliness. Be clean, and the laws of God are on your side. Live in miasma—filth—and you are against the law, and as surely as the lightning strikes the steel, so surely you will suffer. Can anyone doubt, then, with regard to our duty to the poor, who live in places which to breathe in is a rapid death? It is not to level the sties of Bermondsey and St Giles to build fine houses in and to drive the wretched inhabitants to places fouler and more hideous still; but it is to supply baths, water, to clean, and clean, and clean, to purify the rivers, to dig the sewers deep and roof them well, to provide sewerage for the poor, to urge government to obey sanitary laws of old, to tell the rich to give and give till they can cleanse the poor; and what is science for but this?"

ANONYMOUS, "THE GENIUS OF THE REVEREND CHARLES KINGSLEY,"
THE ECLECTIC MAGAZINE OF FOREIGN LITERATURE, SCIENCE, AND ART, 1857

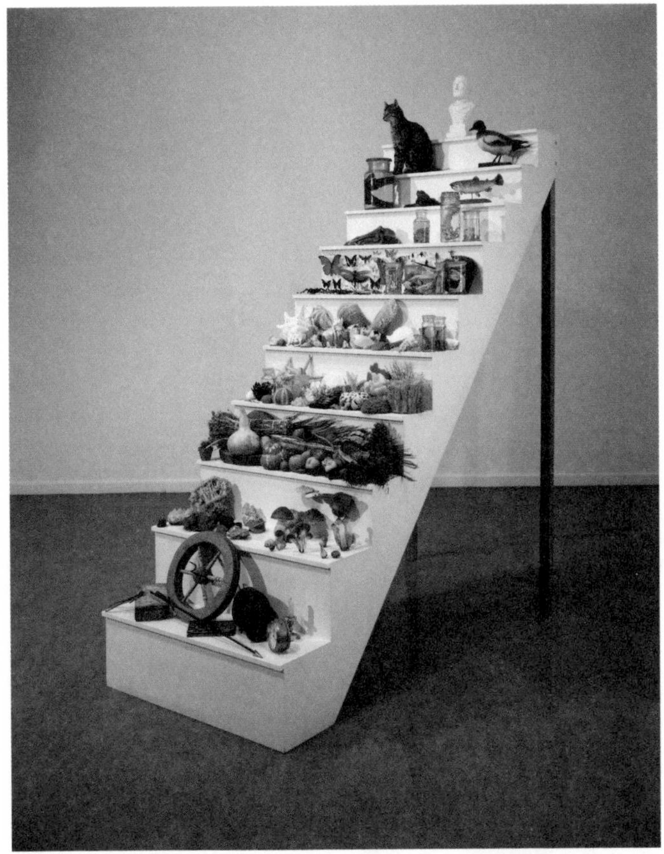

Scala Naturae, 1994

"What is science for, if not to modify the associations of people and things?"

BRUNO LATOUR, *PANDORA'S HOPE*, 1999

Library for the Birds of Massachusetts, 2005

"What is science for, if not to sustain us against the intoxications of night and the temptations exercised by the enchantress appearance?"

VLADIMIR JANKÉLÉVITCH, *MUSIC AND THE INEFFABLE*, 1961

Curiosity Cabinet at the Oceanographic Museum of Monaco, 2011

"The first responsibility of the University is to do its part in answering the gravest of all social questions: *At which end of the ship shall we place the bowsprit?* That is, shall we go forward or backward? Going forward means that we search for the *causes* of undesirable social conditions. This requires us to *do* and not merely discover and *deplore*. When nation-wide defects of economy are joined to nation-wide effects of an unbalanced natural environment, we call to our aid two forces: science and general control for the general good rather than individual control for the individual good. What is science for if not to meet such a situation?"

ISAIAH BOWMAN, "THE TWELVE HOUSES OF HEAVEN," 1941

Bureau of Remote Wildlife Surveillance, 2006

"What is science for, if it does not equip us to face and absorb the shocks of the future?"

INDIRA GANDHI, *SELECTED THOUGHTS*, 1985

Marine Invertebrates, 2013

"What is science for, if not to advise a lethal chamber?"

EMMA GOLDMAN, *THE SOCIAL SIGNIFICANCE OF MODERN DRAMA*, 1914

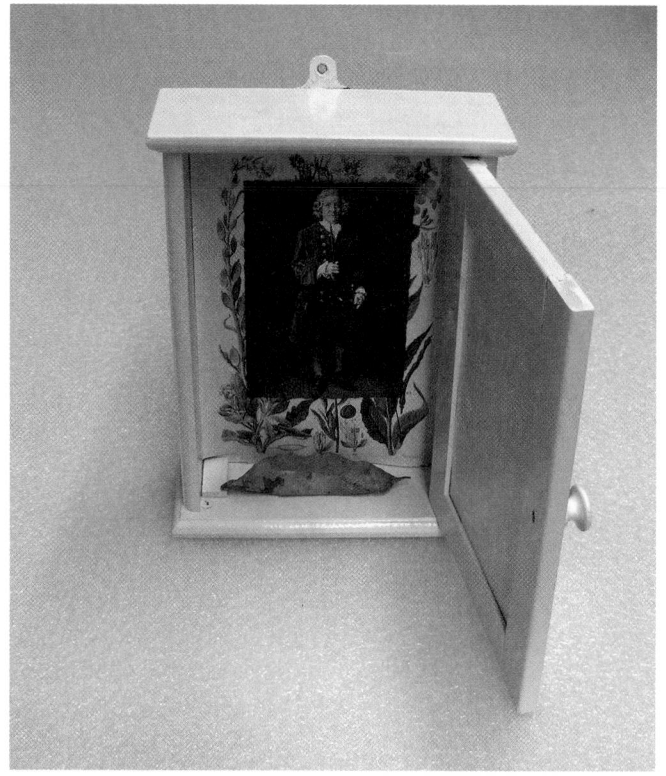

Linnaeus, 1992

"What is science for? When this question is squarely and thoughtfully faced, scientists will agree that science exists for man, and not for itself alone."

U.S. SENATE, "HEARINGS ON SCIENCE LEGISLATION,"
SUBCOMMITTEE ON MILITARY AFFAIRS, 1945

WONDER AND THE ENDS OF INQUIRY

by Lorraine Daston

Science and wonder have a long and ambivalent relationship. Wonder is a spur to scientific inquiry but also a reproach and even an inhibition to inquiry. As philosophers never tire of repeating, only those ignorant of the causes of things wonder: the solar eclipse that terrifies illiterate peasants is no wonder to the learned astronomer who can explain and predict it. Romantic poets accused science of not just neutralizing wonder but of actually killing it. Modern popularizations of science make much of wonder—but expressions of that passion are notably absent in professional publications. This love-hate relationship between wonder and science started with science itself.

Wonder always comes at the beginning of inquiry. "For it is owing to their wonder that men both now begin and at first began to philosophize," explains Aristotle; Descartes made wonder "the first of the passions," and the only one without a contrary, opposing passion. In these and many other accounts of wonder, both soul and senses are ambushed by a puzzle or a surprise, something that catches us unawares and unprepared. Wonder widens the eyes, opens the mouth, stops the heart, freezes thought. Above all, at least in classical accounts like those of Aristotle and Descartes, wonder both diagnoses and cures ignorance. It reveals that there are more things in heaven and earth than have been dreamt of in our philosophy; ideally, it also spurs us on to find an explanation for the marvel.

Therein lies the paradox of wonder: it is the beginning of inquiry (Descartes remarks that people deficient in wonder "are ordinarily quite ignorant"), but the end of inquiry also puts an end to wonder. The marvel that stopped us in our tracks—an aurora borealis, cognate words in languages separated by continents and centuries, the peacock's tail—becomes only an apparent marvel once explained. Aesthetic appreciation may linger (it is no accident that the vernacular descendants of the Latin word for wonder, *admiratio*, convey esteem), but composure has returned. We are delighted but no longer discombobulated; what was once an earthquake of the soul is subdued into an agreeable *frisson*. At least within the classical philosophical tradition, from Aristotle to Descartes (and arguably beyond, to Adam Smith and even to Kant), this negative correlation between wonder and explanation is strong and tenacious. Explanation lies at the heart of the distinction between marvels and miracles in the Latin Christian tradition. What is the difference? Thomas Aquinas answers: marvels (*mirabilia*) are inexplicable to most but not all people (e.g. the eclipse that transfixes the ignorant peasant but not the learned astronomer); miracles (*miracula*) are inexplicable to everyone. Wonder is a barometer of ignorance: the learned experience it rarely; God, never. Wonder is not only a peculiarly human passion; it is also one that, at least on this account, underscores the limits of human knowledge. The more we know, the less we wonder.

This is why wonder was long considered to be a passion at once necessary but ultimately unbecoming to any seeker of knowledge, second only to fear, to which it was closely akin, as a badge of dishonor. Striking a balance between just enough and too much wonder became something of an obsession with early modern philosophers, especially those, like Bacon and Descartes, who were intent on reforming the foundations of natural science. Descartes admitted that wonder was the essential stimulus to inquiry, but fretted that the stimulus could easily become an addictive drug. Excessive wonder (*admiration*) could slide into astonishment (*étonnement*), thereby arresting rather than triggering the quest for explanation. Astonishment, he wrote, "makes the whole body stay immobile like a statue, so that one is unable to perceive any more of the object than the first face presented, nor can one consequently acquire further knowledge of it." A little wonder worked like caffeine upon the mind; too much, more like morphine.

Bacon was similarly ambivalent. On the one hand, he called for the creation of a whole new branch of natural history that would supplement the study of ordinary nature with extraordinary nature: "the errors, vagaries and prodigies of nature, wherein nature deviates and turns aside from her ordinary course." The purpose of this motley collection of all that was "new, rare and unusual" was to chasten rather than to charm. These anomalies would serve as a standing reproach to an Aristotelian natural philosophy unable to deliver explanations of them. Bacon took a dim view of wonders collected simply to please, whether purveyed in books with beguiling titles like *A Thousand Notable Things* or displayed in *Wunderkammern*. His natural history of wonders was meant as a kind of shock therapy to complacent natural philosophers content to study what happens always or most of the time. Yet he was just as skittish as Descartes about overdosing on wonder, which he elsewhere described as "broken knowledge." Wonder was indispensable to inquiry, but only as the spark that ignited the process.

Like eros, wonder was once considered a dangerous passion. Much of the traditional intellectual ambivalence surrounding wonder derived from its affinity to the passions of horror and terror. For us moderns, this link has gone underground, so some excavation is required to make them plausible. Modern wonder, like many of the traditional passions, has faded from the saturated hues of blood red and lapis lazuli blue to baby pink and blue pastels. "Baby" is used advisedly in this context: modern wonder has become infantilized, the stuff of children's entertainment, whether in the form of cartoon fairy tales or science museum exhibitions. Perhaps drawing on wonder's ancient associations with ignorance, modern wonder-mongers address themselves to children or to "the child in all of us." In contrast, premodern wonder was as powerful as dynamite, and just as dangerous. Like anger, wonder has traced a decay curve of declining intensity since Descartes, from passion to emotion. Passions in the original sense of the word (from the Greek *pathema*, the Latin *passio*) are things that we suffer like an illness ("patient" and "passions" share the same root), things that befall rather than move us, not so much states as sieges of the soul. In contrast to the emotions, first conceived in the eighteenth century as movements in the nerves and brain, or the still more delicate sentiments and feelings, passions don't belong to us; we belong to them.

Wonder, horror and terror constitute a trio of passions that has survived the reconceptualization of affect since the late seventeenth century in the works of Descartes, Hume, Adam Smith, Kant, Rousseau, Darwin, William James and many others. This

Phil Ross, from *Pure Culture*, 1998-2005
Ganoderma lucidum fungi

trio is unusual in at least three respects. First, all three contain a distinctly cognitive component. In order to feel horror, terror or wonder, one must first register an anomaly: these are the observant passions, which pick out the extraordinary against the background of the ordinary. Second, although all three deserve to be called vehement with respect to their intensity, they are not single-minded. The perceived anomalies that trigger wonder or horror or terror are so far beyond the usual range of experience that doubt vies with recognition in the mind: these are the I-can't-believe-my-eyes passions, which split the self into skeptic and believer. Third, and most important for my purposes, the anomalies that evoke this trio of passions are violations of order. They are the passions of the unnatural.

Horror, terror and wonder are triggered when a major disruption of order (whether moral or natural or both) is registered as such: an act of perception and judgment that presumes some acquaintance with the particular sort of orderliness that has been breached—that, as the phrase goes, "something is not right." Subterranean connections bind the passions of the unnatural to each other. Although, for example, horror and wonder may seem poles apart as states of experience, they are linked by deep ties, as evidenced by the strange tendency of one passion to tip over into the other—for example in responses to monsters. Horror and terror are more obviously related to one another, but the peculiar terror evoked by natural disasters also shows revealing affinities to wonder. Despite dramatic differences in emotional texture, wonder, terror and horror all contain a moment of astonished disbelief. They are the eye-rubbing passions of incredulity: Can this really be happening? These passions form a triplet, united both by their interrelationships and by a shared tendency to blur moral and natural stimuli. They are the subjective side of the objective perception of a disorder so dramatic that even nature quakes.

Against this background, the traditional philosophical ambivalence toward wonder becomes intelligible: wonder may, like horror and terror, be triggered by an anomaly begging for rational explanation, but it can all too easily, like horror and terror, paralyze reason. That wonder always bordered on religious awe did not improve its reputation among the party of reason, whether peopled by premodern philosophers or modern scientists. Indeed the fact that naturalists since the Pre-Socratics have made precisely those phenomena most likely to evoke awe and appeals to the divine—such as thunder, eclipses and earthquakes—their primary explananda strongly suggest that killing wonder was not simply the by-product of natural inquiry; it was its aim.

Many humanists nowadays still suspect scientists of being wonder-killers. They echo Romantics like Wordsworth, who complained about the kind of natural philosopher (the word "scientist" was not introduced into English until the 1830s) who would "peep and botanize / Upon his mother's grave," or the melancholy anti-modernism of a whole gaggle of twentieth-century social thinkers, most of them Central European, who equated the rise of scientific and technological rationality (which they rarely bothered to distinguish) with "disenchantment" (Max Weber), loss of a cozy *Lebenswelt* (Edmund Husserl), or "the disappearance of the cosmos" (Alexandre Koyré). These elegies for a lost world spangled with marvels and hushed with the wonder of it all fly in the teeth of both historical fact and daily experience: it is popular science and science fiction that feed the modern public's hunger for wonders, handily outselling books about the Shroud of Turin and the healing miracles of Lourdes. But perhaps all these wonders of popular science are just that: wonders for popular consumption. What about the actual doing of science? In this context, wonder has undergone three major transformations.

First, wonder is strongly associated with *hoi polloi*, at least in publications. Whereas exclamations of wonder were quite common in works of astronomy and natural history and not unknown in philosophy and philology throughout the eighteenth and early nineteenth century, they are increasingly scarce thereafter. The professionalization of the scholar and scientist as salaried university professors during this period has long been associated with the rise of ostentatious sobriety and the cult of expertise. The association of wonder with ignorance, and still more with the ignorance of children, accorded ill with both. Yet wonder never vanished from the writings of scientists and scholars: like the return of the repressed, it overflows from the pages of their autobiographies and memoirs, not just their popular books addressed to a mass audience. Albert Einstein's anecdote about the two wonders of his childhood that steered him toward a scientific career, the magnet and Euclidean geometry, is typical of the genre.

Second, the nature of what counts as wondrous has changed, in this case already in the early Enlightenment. Einstein's two wonders are emblematic of wonders before and after. Since Antiquity the lodestone has been part of the canon of wonders—and its mysterious powers of attraction and repulsion threw down the gauntlet to natural philosophers to come up with a sturdy explanation. But Euclidean geometry, although almost as ancient, most certainly did not qualify as one of Bacon's prodigies, despite the fact that it was roundly and resoundingly admired by early-modern savants from Galileo to Spinoza. What Einstein marveled at was the harvest of surprising conclusions derived from so few and such self-evident premises: the wonder did not cry out for explanation; the wonder *was* the explanation. The transfer of wonder from the beginning to the end of inquiry was already well underway by the mid-eighteenth century, which celebrated Newton's magisterial synthesis of celestial and terrestrial mechanics as the achievement of a demigod, and had become a *fait accompli* by the time Darwin published *On the Origin of Species* in 1859, the final pages of which also invoked the wonder of "this view of life." (The humanities were by no means devoid of such epiphanies, e.g. the reconstruction of the family tree of Indo-European languages, the inspiration for Darwin's similar tree-like diagram of modification with descent in the *Origin*.) What merited wonder in all these cases was a synthesis that unified apparently disparate phenomena within a single explanatory scheme—the tides and the orbits of the planets; oviparous birds and oviparous dinosaurs; Sanskrit and Latin. Wonder was the fruit, not just the seed of inquiry, the too-good-to-be-true surprise that so many apparently diverse things could all be explained so economically.

Third, the complexion of wonder paled. I have already sketched the trajectory of wonder from passion to emotion, with its consequent loss of intensity and also of menace. By the time Burke and Kant were writing on the sublime in the late eighteenth century, fear had been mostly drained from the

Phil Ross, from *Pure Culture*, 1998-2005
Ganoderma lucidum fungi

wondrous. Kant even went so far as to make a slight tremor of fear followed by the reassurance of perfect safety a component of the sublime. Only in rare moments of existential danger, usually in connection with devastating hurricanes, volcanoes or other natural disasters, does wonder assert itself at full strength, once again reunited with its boon companions horror and terror. But for the most part, modern wonder has lost its power to terrify, and with it, much of its power *tout court*. Modern museum reconstructions of Renaissance princely *Wunderkammern* do capture their delightful hodge-podgery—the stuffed crocodile next to the cherrystone carved with a thousand faces next to a nautilus shell garlanded in gold—but they cannot recapture the politics of shock and awe with which the Hapsburgs in Prague or the Sforzas in Milan hoped to cow diplomats and potentates visiting such collections. Modern wonder, whether evoked by an animated movie for children or by the latest NASA photographs from the Mars probe, bears approximately the same relationship to premodern wonder as the chubby cupids featured on valentines do to the Eros whose arrows doomed Pasiphaë and Phaedra to impossible loves. It no longer requires the full armamentarium of philosophy to combat such a tame creature.

What consequences do these transformations of wonder have for inquiry? First, they have affected the sciences and the humanities in almost equal measure. If anything, humanists are even more chary of expressing wonder in their scholarly publications or even their popular ones. To do so flirts with vulgarity, even kitsch. Second, although wonder, or at least a certain raised-eyebrow surprise, may still initiate inquiry, scholars and scientists reserve their mingled wonder and admiration for the outcome. Third, in contrast to the copious, various aesthetic of the *Wunderkammer*, wonder now accrues to revelations of deep unity underlying apparent miscellany. Wonder is now not only reserved for the end of inquiry; it is evoked by almost the opposite stimuli. The end of inquiry is no longer to make wonder stop, but to let it begin.

Eve Andrée Laramée, *Ingredients*, 2001

IN PRAISE OF THINGS

by Lily Huang

Occasionally I have the pleasure of being arrested by some earnest phrase in a work of science that takes a part of the world and sets it moving. This happened when I read, for instance, a sober reflection in a book of evolutionary biology on the fortunes of the earliest cells: "Fusion results in an immediate increase in size. An increase in size surely acts as a buffer against a wide variety of size-related sources of mortality." Also this statement, from a biogeography textbook: "Areas of endemism in Central America correspond very closely for birds, reptiles, and amphibians, but much less so when butterflies are involved." These are gleeful moments for me: they reorient parts of the world—some place where an investigator might pronounce the cause of death to be the victim's size; or some affair in which "butterflies are involved." Before these encounters, the ideas perturbed by them had been fixed to the firmament under which I daily walk about: they were undifferentiated portions of the mundane totality of facts, which for the most part I ignore, assuming out of habit that this is not where the action is—not the loose hem where the world is still in the midst of changing. But then an idea, a mere word, quivers in some unexpected recombination, and I am reminded that, contrary to a certain humanistic prejudice, a fact is a living thing. Though pinned in some fashion—hustled into a word, pressed into a gridded curve—a fact remains in motion. To think, with panicked humanists past and present, that science fixes the world in place and deadens the imagination is to come to a rash conclusion both about facts and about death. Even fossils, after all, are "not done with their changes."

This rashness comes of a rather aged indignation, traceable to at least one respectable source. It was Keats, himself a formidable metamorphysician, who mixed lament with insult and set the tenor of the resistance against the sterility of natural philosophy:

> ... Do not all charms fly
> At the mere touch of cold philosophy?
> There was an awful rainbow once in heaven:
> We know her woof, her texture; she is given
> In the dull catalogue of common things.

We can certainly choose, by these lines, to cleave the world in two—two visions, two kinds of explanation, two kinds of imaginative life. We can read Keats's poem as a definitive statement that natural philosophy is essentially and irrevocably the antithesis of poetry—that it has nothing poetic about it. I choose not to: I cannot accept a categorical denunciation of the duller rainbow, for such a reading would constrain science and poetry alike. To read this way would be to meet the world in the same cataloguing spirit that Keats despised. It is against the spirit of poetry to be so choosy: for poetry to determine in advance the province of dullness amounts to a poetic dogmatism as unbecoming as the purported scientific one.

But we have fortified our acceptance of scientific dullness in another way. That objectionable coldness of touch, said Weber, becomes great capability: unfettered by myth, heedless of grace, the scientific intellect may truly come to master the world's rattling contents. The secular catalogue is eminently useful precisely for being dull, and if we lose by it a rather beautiful but antiquated enchantment, such is our wizened lot. We shall have things, not gods.

Take this, then, as a different defense of things: a defense of complex hydraulics, and hard carbon, and of the "businesslike atom"; of musculature, secretions, surgical scalpels; of our "apish cousins"; the unicorn of the sea; and that "albino giraffe," the sycamore tree; of the "capillaries of the delta" and the "waves of chlorophyll in motion." Take this as a reminder of all poets who have read that dull catalogue with feeling, and felt no antipathy toward the science of those objects, nor toward scientific labor, but instead perceived in that endeavor a companion effort to put the world into words.

The grace of things is that they should bear names; over this Hopkins spent his life in rapture. Auden met him at that altar, but the fellow pilgrim he chose to recognize there was Keats. Lecturing at Oxford in 1956, Auden described the existence of a certain cast of things that had a particular bearing on his life as a poet. He called these things Sacred Objects and Sacred Beings, and explained the way they invited the poetic imagination into a particular communion.

> The impression made upon the imagination by any sacred being is of an overwhelming but undefinable importance—an unchangeable quality, an Identity, as Keats said: I-am-that-I-am is what every sacred being seems to say.

There is a sense, in these encounters, that the imagination is held captive by sacredness: it does not so much create as receive. Yet despite the distant echo of God's own speech, the encounter between the sacred and the imagination is not exactly enlightening. It is not a moment of clarity for the poet, nor of resolution. Rather, it is the opposite: the *beginning* of a mystery, the discovery of an unidentified nerve in the world, alive with meaning, as compelling as it is vague. "A sacred being cannot be anticipated," said Auden, "it must be encountered. On encounter the imagination has no option but to respond." Its response "is a passion of awe."

The things that struck the boy Auden in this way mostly had to do with lead mining. He was obsessed with the burial of ore and the precise means of extraction; with the necessary design of machinery; with, in fact, the whole north of England—where the mining districts were—and the particular names of the underground veins open there for mining. He read more technical literature than storybooks, and hardly any poetry besides the Psalms and the hymnal. But: "Looking back," he said, "I now realize that I had read the technological prose of my favorite books in a peculiar way. A word like *pyrites*, for example, was for me not simply an indicative sign; it was the Proper Name of a Sacred Being."

"Proper names," Auden wrote in *A Certain World*, "are poetry in the raw." The commonplace book he published in 1970, *A Certain World* is an autobiography with the central figure removed, or never constituted; it marks the path of an undeclared walker. We guess the spirit by its stopping-places. A lengthy section follows the heading "Proper Names" and the first entry is a solemn observation of Thoreau's: "With knowledge of the name comes a distincter recognition and knowledge of the thing." Why this should be—why the name of something should bestow depth and clarity to the thing itself—

returns to the central enigma of this story of poetic grace. The propriety of a given name comes from the name's being *of* the thing—in the words of Coleridge, such a name "always partakes of the Reality which it renders intelligible." For Coleridge the highest language consisted of "symbols consubstantial with truths." Words could be, as they once were, "living powers"—not the mere husks of things, not sepulchres of thought and feeling. They are vessels, to be sure, but they too are in motion, and they are part of what they convey, like Ezekiel's "living chariot." Auden put it this way:

> Language is prosaic to the degree that it does not matter what particular word is associated with an idea, provided the association once made is permanent. Language is poetic to the degree that it does matter.

What is striking, too, about poetic sacredness is how little the identity of the poet has to do with it. Auden's autobiography is a constellation around an invisible axis. That "unchangeable attribute" that Keats so admired, which is none other than the quality of being a self, is absent in the poet. What distinguishes the poet from every other being, animate and inanimate alike, is exactly what makes him so very hard to distinguish. The poet, writes Keats, "has no character"—is, in fact, "the most unpoetical of any thing in existence." But he "lives in gusto, be it foul or fair," for he is a "camelion" who takes on the character of all other things. This is his "negative capability," the ability to inhabit other entities to perfection, with no possibility of any residue of himself, for he is no positive quantity at all. "Continually ... filling some other body," he sees with eyes not his own and speaks always through others.

If Auden's poet is a figure struck still by its encounters, Keats's poet is an undiscriminating breath of air passing through the world, an obedient Ariel. Both are more severe forms of self-effacement than the scientist's. In an encounter with a Sacred Object, the imagination has no choice but to let the object speak. It takes a self-stilled, self-negating poet to recognize this native speech, and the poem that follows is misunderstood if it is taken as a song of the poet's self—it is really a song of all other selves. Thus Hopkins listened to what "each tucked string tells," how "each hung bell's / Bow swung finds tongue to fling out broad its name"—

> Each mortal thing does one thing and the same:
> Deals out that being indoors each one dwells;
> Selves—goes its self; *myself* it speaks and spells,
> Crying *What I do is me: for that I came.*

With the name come the self-declaring actions—the catching fire, the drawing flame—the whole being dealing itself out. The poet is not expressing himself; he is approximating as best he can the echo of the object. "Dapple-dáwn-drawn Falcon, in his riding / of the rolling level underneath him steady air": that echoing name hovers too, as a being that is brighter than the day bursts from its surroundings—out of the prosaic sky, out of the unpoetic condition of being unperceived. It is the poet's perceiving that sets the thing free, reveals it wheeling, lets it have its say: "AND the fire that breaks from thee then...!" Such, then, is the objectivity of poets.

Poetry and science aid each other in the work of perceiving, in setting things in motion. Both are in attendance at the stirring of

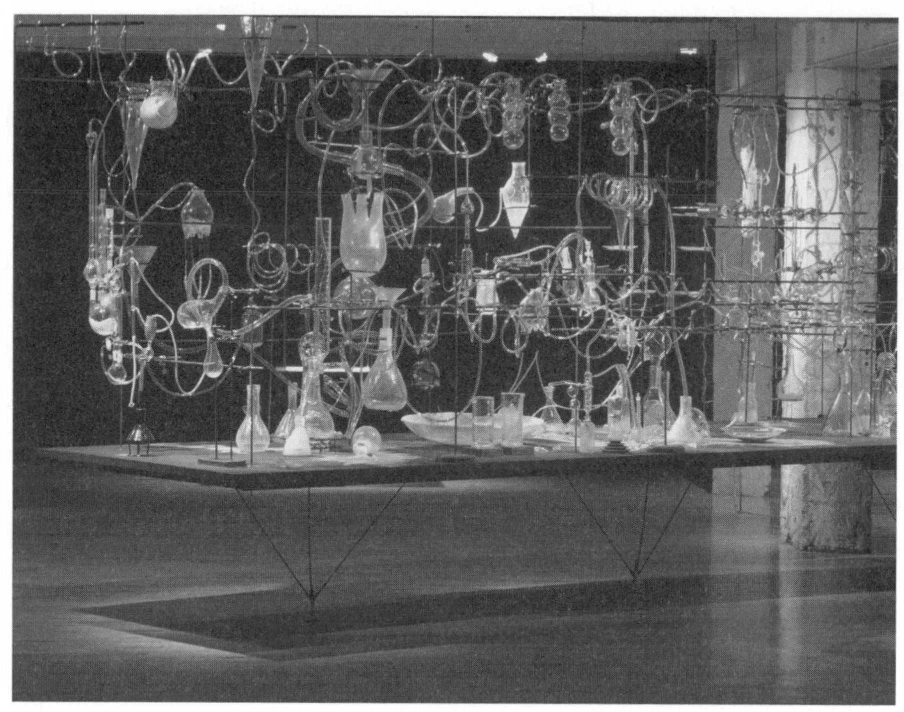

Eve Andrée Laramée, *Apparatus for the Distillation of Vague Intuitions*, 2001

objects into sacredness—into communion with the imagination—and they do not, I think, simply attend the same phenomenon in contrary spirits. The words by which science comes to know things have manners and movements intrinsic to them as poetic names do. Even a scientific understanding of constitutive processes or parts—the dreaded woof and texture of things—can lend an object a more pronounced identity, more ways to "deal out being." Is it disenchanting to discover what the summit of Mount Everest is made of? Auden, presumably, would have been happy to learn of any new rock, but what awe would have seized him to find one there that he already knew—marine limestone, its name conveying it all the way from the sea?

Do we ever obliterate a thing by defining it? Only when it is a bad definition. With a name a thing comes to life—a premise so basic to poetry that it cannot be from poets that the charge of intellectual anesthetization comes. When we say that the earth moves in plates, and the air moves in cells, in what way are we disassembling the world, rather than continuing the work of perceiving? When we call the air sucked from a mountaintop by gravity "katabatic winds"? I have heard the stegosaurus's plates described as "radiators," for they are filled with blood vessels and angled to face the sun—a lizard-heater. "Glacial dust" is the parched leavings of a retreating glacier—not to be confused with "marine snow," the speck-sized remainders of animals falling, slowly but inexorably, to the bottom of the ocean, bound, if they are not picked away, for the residents of the "hadal communities." And it is not only underwater dust that falls: D'Arcy Thompson described the life of the tiny creatures called diatoms and foraminifera as a single drawn-out fall through the ocean, of "exceeding slowness."

"How the needle of nature delighteth to work, even in low and doubtful vegetations," wrote one who walked leisurely along the curves of sentences, Sir Thomas Browne. Science makes objects out of such lowly things, scopes poised and taking names. If science fixes the things of this world, it is only to see more scrupulously their finer changes. Just one man may serve to illustrate: Darwin, bent over his potted earthworms, sifting and weighing their small excretions, and perceiving geologic change in those tremblings of dust, the loamy layer growing, the earth loosening, millimeter by millimeter.

THE SOVIET SCIENCE SYSTEM

by Michael D. Gordin

Gather a crowd of historians and philosophers of science into a room and ask them to define "science." On second thought, don't try this at home, because you'd likely meet with stony-faced refusal on the part of the first and raucous disagreement from the second. Yet isn't the task rather straightforward? Isn't this just another classic instance of academics creating mountains out of molehills? Actually, no. The problem is fiendishly frustrating (and likely intractable) simply because of the kind of activity science actually turns out to be in practice.

Consider, for example, what it clearly isn't. Science cannot be simply a collection of true propositions about nature. Most of what has counted uncontroversially as "science" during the past few centuries—geocentric astronomy, phlogiston chemistry, ether physics, the inheritance of acquired characteristics—is now considered to be false. Even worse, much of what we *now* consider to be science is doubtless going to be proven false, since nature was unkind enough to deny us the answer key. Science is also not merely the proper execution of method, both because various disciplines display a whole hodgepodge of different methods, and also because one can apply all the accepted methodology and come up with doctrines (parapsychology, eugenics, phrenology) that we would with alacrity exclude. The problem gets worse when you go farther back in time or across cultures. Mayan astronomy, Classical Chinese alchemy, Hippocratic medicine—all these are rather distinct from what we now consider to be "science," and yet it strikes most scholars as rather churlish to dismiss them. No one has been able to come up with a broadly consensual definition of science, and I am certainly not about to do so here.

Nonetheless, science seems as easy to identify as pornography was in the immortal characterization of Justice Potter Stewart: you know it when you see it. Why are we so confident that we recognize science? A major reason is that the elite natural sciences—by which I mean physics, chemistry, biology, geology and so on—resemble each other very strongly in their external features, however much they differ from each other in terms of theories, practices, fashions and organization of research (some in the lab, some in the field, some at the blackboard and most at a computer at some point during the day). The homogeneity is striking. Knowledge in these domains is communicated largely by articles and conference papers, not books. The journals *Science* and *Nature* sit at the apex of a byzantine hierarchy of periodicals that parse the disciplines and subdisciplines, and articles in almost every field display a standardized template (Introduction, Methods, Results and Discussion, a.k.a. IMRAD), entombed in the passive voice and simplified clause structure. The language of these communications is English; Russian, German, French and Japanese shrank to statistical insignificance decades ago. Postdocs cycle from Calcutta to Capetown to Cardiff to Columbus, and the laboratories they enter at each site, the journals they download to their laptops, the language they speak when they enter their new workplaces—all exhibit the familiarity of the only science they have ever known.

But this predictable uniformity has nothing to do with "truth" or "nature" or "scientific method." These are the hallmarks not of science itself, but rather of what we might call a "science system." In today's world there is only one of these. It resembles largely (but not wholly) that developed in the United States after World War II, and it is simply how science "is done" today, no matter where you happen to be. That's how we believe we know it when we see it: it is hard to conceive of science otherwise, because we are not regularly confronted with instances from a different system. But not too long ago, there was not one science system in the world, but two. A sojourn around the landscape of the second system—what I will dub the Soviet Science System—reveals an organization of expertise of the natural world that strikes us as undeniably science, but not as we know it.

•

Expertise is not organized neutrally; in fact, it is hard to imagine what a "neutral" organization of expertise would look like. Experts are organized *for* something, which means a decision—usually political—about appropriate goals, and experts must be organized to fit ideologically and institutionally within the broader culture and polity. The annoying thing about experts is, well, their *expertise.* Not everyone has it, or the opportunity to acquire it: it's expensive to train people, and nature does not distribute competence equally. For a Communist country like the former Union of Soviet Socialist Republics, the problem of experts was perpetually aggravating, and periodically burst into flame. (The same is true, by the by, for the American system: pointy-headed elites fare poorly at moments of populist politicking—witness the periodic Climategates—and centralized federal money after World War II aggravated partisans of states' rights decentralization.) The Soviet Science System presented one enormously influential solution to the perpetual problem of expertise—and then it vanished. Mostly.

Yet there was no single Soviet Science System. The structures that began to coalesce under the ramshackle regime controlled by Vladimir Lenin from a nineteenth-century European-style precursor was rather distinct from the one that Joseph Stalin consolidated beginning in 1928. Nikita Khrushchev in the 1950s de-Stalinized some aspects of the science system and left others intact. The most stable era of the Soviet Science System lasted from 1965 to 1991, spanning the slowly disintegrating Soviet Union from Leonid Brezhnev to Mikhail Gorbachev. (Some aspects of it continue—or are even being resurrected—under Vladimir Putin.) As with time, so also for space: the System manifested differently in Siberia as compared to the Baltics, acquired specific aspects in Moscow as opposed to Leningrad.

If we zoom in on the details, we'll be lost before we begin. Let's focus on the tapestry as a whole instead of the exquisite needlework. The primary notion to keep in mind is that any science system is primarily for organizing expertise, and that is a tale of ends (what is science for?) and means (how do we get there?). Translated into the Soviet Science System, this suggests we look at ideology and scale.

•

"Ideology" is a squishy term. In what follows, I will take it as given that everyone has an ideology, in the capacious sense of a set of principles (conscious or not) by which one makes sense of one's surroundings. Scientists have ideology too, and the Western science system is shot through with it: flexible, mobile labor; double-blind peer review; competitive funding—these are not ideology-free (regardless of whether they are desirable). The difference with the Soviet system is that there the ideology, Marxism-Leninism, was explicit, although its precise interpretation went through rather dramatic transformations over its 74-year lifespan.

Marxism-Leninism applied to science was called "dialectical materialism," and despite now having a somewhat malodorous reputation, it is actually a fairly presentable philosophy of science. As a materialism, it rules out vital forces, spiritual essences, souls—the vestiges of nineteenth-century *Naturphilosophie*. The dialectics part means that nature (or the perceptual apparatus by which we apprehend nature) behaves in a certain manner, such as through a transition from changes in quantity to changes in quality (think periodic table: add an identical proton and get a wholly different chemical element).

Dialectical materialism was official, so in principle every scientist in the Soviet Union either propounded it explicitly or at the very least didn't spout off about logical positivism or other bourgeois nonsense. Marxism was *scientific* socialism, and science had a uniquely significant status in the Communist cosmology. Courses in dialectical materialism were required of all university students, and superficial adherence to its tenets was enforced. As Americans penned their IMRAD articles (themselves structured around an ideological frame of neo-positivism), the Soviets publicly displayed conformity in technical papers on quantum electrodynamics or geomorphology through ritual invocations of the epistemological insights of Lenin or Engels (or, before the de-Stalinization of the mid-1950s, Stalin himself).

To us, having an "official philosophy of science" just sounds plain weird, and it has been the source of much mockery of Soviet science, by both Westerners and its former practitioners. But if you teach a whole nation a powerful philosophy of science, some of them might find it useful. Vladimir A. Fock (1898-1974) reported that his engagement with the ideology enabled him to devise a new set of harmonic coordinates for general relativity. Yakov I. Frenkel (1894-1952) developed his notion of "holes" and "collective excitations" in condensed-matter physics through extensive reflection on contemporary Soviet political thought. And it is impossible to read the theories of psychologist Lev Vygotsky (1896-1934) about the development of language in children—currently ascendant in cognitive psychology over Jean Piaget's stage model—without observing how his notion of a social language explicates a distinctively Marxist position. These are all reasonable scientific theories whose origins are rooted in ideology.

Ideology mattered in other ways at the state level. When Khrushchev abandoned Stalin's "socialism in one country" for the less confrontational but equally competitive "peaceful coexistence," he also promoted a cosmonaut program designed not so much to bury the West as to demonstrate the superiority of Soviet methods for organizing knowledge. (The United States in turn promoted its own space program globally as the hallmark of Americanism.) In all these

Alejandro Guijarro, *Stanford* from *Momentum* series, 2010-2013

instances, ideology helped set the agenda for the organization of expertise, what expertise was supposed to be *for*.

It had a dark side, as these things often do. In the Soviet ideological frame, nature existed for the sake of exploitation by humans to build a better society, thus promoting catastrophic environmental degradation in the service of modernization—most graphically instantiated in the 1986 Chernobyl reactor meltdown. Content followed the same pattern as context. For example, in the late 1930s Vygotsky's theories were suppressed as ideological heresy, replaced by decades of behaviorism. Or consider the most notorious episode in the history of Soviet science: the "Lysenko Affair." In the late 1920s, a young Ukrainian-born agronomist named Trofim Lysenko began promoting a program he called *iarovizatsiia* ("vernalization" in the standard English translation), procedures like rubbing seeds with ice in order to enhance their viability during cold winters. Interestingly, this really works—in fact, it was not even a discovery, being already a much-discussed phenomenon among plant physiologists. Lysenko's innovation, assisted by several canny advisors, was to promote vernalization as part of a biological system he called "Michurinism," a Marxist-friendly theory of heredity. Soviet philosophers' problems with genetics were both ontological ("genes" were ideal, immaterial phantasms dreamed up by an Augustinian friar) and political (if heredity was unchangeable, there was little room for progress). According to Lysenko, the procedures of vernalization "shattered" the hereditary material of plants, transmuting a somatic shock into a transmissible trait—in short, the inheritance of acquired characteristics, vestiges of Jean-Baptiste Lamarck's long-dismissed theory. Genes, Lysenko maintained, were pseudoscientific.

A vigorous debate between Michurinists and geneticists raged during the 1930s, quieted down in the early 1940s—but not before the leading Soviet geneticist, Nikolai Vavilov, was arrested and sent to a prison camp; he died of malnutrition in 1943—and then resurfaced with a vengeance in 1948. In August of that year, during the last session of a conference at the All-Union Lenin Institute of Agricultural Sciences that Lysenko had usurped from Vavilov in the internecine warfare characteristic of many science systems, Lysenko announced that Joseph Stalin had endorsed Michurinism. Genetics was proscribed. Stalin died five years later, but Lysenko held on at the pinnacle of Soviet biology until 1965, when the geneticists emerged from the sheltering protection of nuclear bomb-designers (in whose institutes their research had been coded as "radiation biology") and dethroned him. The era was an utter catastrophe for Soviet biology, which had to painfully resurrect the science of genetics.

Yet this most scandalous of displays within the Soviet Science System was also quite atypical. Periodically, would-be Lysenkos emerged from the woodwork, sporting dialectical-materialist slogans and seeking state backing, and almost always they failed. In the meantime, the Soviet Union produced some of the most brilliant physics, mathematics and geology of the twentieth century. The Soviet Science System had pathologies, but they were just that: pathologies. They were not the ordinary course of affairs, and most individuals functioned in the system undamaged by the Law of the Negation of the Negation or Friedrich Engels's views on energeticism. In the end, no matter what you did, ideology framed the way you did it—how could it not?

•

Once ideology has framed the ends, the science system must confront the problem of *means*. In the Soviet Science System, this was a matter of scale, which was then molded into institutions.

Had alien anthropologists voyaged to Earth fifty years ago to see how humans organized their knowledge of nature, scale alone would have drawn them Sovietward. The Soviet Union spanned one-sixth of the planet's land surface, and the Soviet Science System was even larger, spreading beyond its borders to the Communist bloc—Eastern Europe, China, North Korea, Cuba—and even to those regions of the globe that were once called the "Third World" (especially India, Egypt and parts of Latin America). On every level, the Soviet Science System liked things big.

Even if you recall next to nothing about the Soviet Union's technical achievements, you likely know two things: the launching of the first artificial satellite, Sputnik, in October 1957; and the emergence of the Soviet Union as the second nuclear superpower after its first atomic test in August 1949. Both space and nukes dominated the foreign image of Soviet science and technology (massive arsenals, Yuri Gagarin as the first man in space, nuclear submarines and so on), but the bigness had a domestic face as well: enormous dam and canal projects, the construction of an expansive spur to the Trans-Siberian Railway through intractable permafrost, electrification of the countryside and more.

The Soviet Science System did things on a gigantic scale because that is what it was set up for. It had the cadres for it. In 1991, the last year of the Soviet Union, state statistics counted more than 1.5 million scientific researchers. Official Soviet numbers should always be taken with a grain of salt, but external estimates consistently placed the quantity of Soviet scientists and engineers as ten to thirty percent greater than in the United States. With enormous labor at its disposal (some of it forced Gulag labor) and a lackadaisical relationship to punctilious bookkeeping, Soviet planners often disregarded human, financial and environmental costs in the interests of grand planning. The painful and murderous construction of the Belomor Canal between the Baltic and the White Seas is one infamous instance. (If you consider canal building "engineering" and not "science," see above about ideology.) Another never-implemented Stalinist project proposed reversing the flow of northward-bound Soviet rivers through multiple "peaceful nuclear explosions" across Siberia in order to address the falling water levels of the Aral Sea, itself a consequence of massive cotton plantations across Central Asia. Bigness begat more bigness, and the knowledge system operated the same way.

The institutions also had to be big. If the American Science System during the Cold War rivaled the Soviet in terms of scale per capita, at the administrative level the Soviet system exhibited features utterly foreign to bourgeois eyes. Dominating this knowledge bureaucracy was the Academy of Sciences of the Soviet Union. The Soviet Academy was no honorific learned society to which individuals were named when they reached the summit of their research careers at institutions of higher education. Teaching was done at Soviet universities, but teaching was the only thing universities did. The Academy was a purely research institution, the universities entirely pedagogical. This way the country's leading researchers wouldn't be bothered by pesky undergraduates and could fully devote themselves to science. The Academy distributed research funds to those within its hallowed domain, line items in a titanic budget that came as part of the job rather than as the result of a competitive peer-reviewed process—wasteful duplication of resources, from the Soviet point of view—and researchers spent their entire lives from graduate-education cradle to senescent grave within the bosom of specialized research. With constant research funds, permanent employment and no obligation to teach, Soviet scientists were free from the frictions of the Americanized research university framework.

The Academy had started rather differently. In 1724, Tsar Peter I (also known as "the Great," although the appropriateness of that moniker is one of the most debated questions of Russian history) capped a series of reforms of every aspect of Russian governance—civil service, military organization, taxation, the alphabet and even the location of the capital—by creating an Imperial Academy of Sciences. There were as yet no Russians trained to function at the elite level of European natural philosophy, so the ranks of academicians were staffed largely by Central Europeans recommended by Gottfried Leibniz's disciple Christian Wolff (among them Leonhard Euler, who would become the most illustrious mathematician of the century). The academicians published in Latin, a recent import to this decisively non-Catholic land, and chattered away in German. Over the course of the eighteenth century, Latin faded but German persisted, and Russians recruited from a fledgling university system began to populate this scientific Olympus. (The rolls of the Academy were distinguished, although Russian savants familiar to us like Dmitrii Mendeleev and Nikolai Lobachevsky were denied access to its pastures.) Publications from the Academy continued to issue forth in international tongues like German and French, but Russian emerged by the end of the nineteenth century as preferred. The Imperial Academy was, in short, much like the Académie des sciences in Paris or the Prussian Akademie der Wissenschaften in Berlin: part honorific, part research, all prestige.

The Revolution of 1917 did not change this much. Academicians, like Russian intellectuals at large, ranged in conviction from blue-blooded monarchists to British-style liberals, and generally did not welcome Lenin's socialist republic. Yet they didn't lobby against it either, and the most influential of them, like Ivan Pavlov (think dogs, bells, drool), used his international prestige to better scholars' wretched living conditions during the painful years of civil war. The rupture came early in Stalin's reign, as young Bolsheviks railed against the privileges of this counter-revolutionary elite. Foreign specialists who had been consulting on industrial expansion in the mining and railroad industries were prosecuted as "wreckers," and "red specialists" came into ascendancy. In 1929 the Academy was "bolshevized": expanded to admit more scholars with pliant politics to dilute the possibility of this venerable institution becoming a venerable liability. With one hand Stalin took away, with another he gave: heaps of resources and mountains of status.

Alejandro Guijarro, *Cambridge* from *Momentum* series, 2010-2013

From being a classic indicator of reactionary politics in the 1920s, by the 1950s "academician" was one of the most prestigious titles in the Soviet pantheon.

The Academy was gargantuan. The All-Union Academy had branches in Moscow, Leningrad and eventually Novosibirsk, as well as specialized institutions, ecological reservations and laboratories scattered everywhere. The fifteen constituent republics of the Soviet Union had their own Academies of Sciences, a mini-Olympus to mirror the structures of the Union. Ukraine got the first clone in 1918, then Belorussia in 1929 and then a deluge starting in 1941, as Stalin mobilized for the war and then re-mobilized for the postwar: loyal Georgia in 1941, but also newly annexed Lithuania, fruit of the Hitler-Stalin pact; all the way to Kyrgyzstan in 1954, the year after the *vozhd*'s demise. (Did I say fifteen? I meant fourteen. There was one republic within the Soviet Union that never got its own academy: the Russian Soviet Federal Socialist Republic. This despite the fact that most institutions of the "All-Union" Academy were based on its territory. The oversight became a sticking point with Russian nationalists in the late 1980s and contributed to anti-Soviet mobilization.) Academies on the Soviet model were erected or restructured across the Communist world. Even the Prussian Academy of Sciences, located after World War II in the German Democratic Republic, was reshaped by the end of the 1960s into a massive research complex. Replication was a characteristic of the Soviet Science System, reproducing the same structures of funding, training, employment, intellectual property (or lack thereof) and publishing wherever it spread.

The Academy and its unfortunate stepbrothers the universities were not the only institutions of science, of course, and I mention a few others only in passing because we know far less about them. The KGB had its own scientific institutions, reviewing the competence as well as the loyalty of scholars. During Stalin's time engineering shops (known as *sharashki*) were set up within the prison system, and prison labor was instrumental in the construction of the atomic and space megaliths. The largest parallel institution to the Academy, however, was the military, which controlled "closed cities" dotted across the map—or not quite, since they were erased from the maps to keep prying eyes out. Each of these was part of the structure to organize expertise, a structure molded closely to the shifting demands of politics and society.

•

So that was the Soviet Science System, in a nutshell. But was "Soviet science" truly a species of the genus *science*, or simply some horrific bastardization that had nothing to do with the pursuit of knowledge? Let us return to Potter Stewart's maxim: we know science when we see it. Did the Soviet Science System look like science? Most definitely. And it produced loads of knowledge too, much of it still considered foundational: the Moscow School of Mathematics, Lev Landau's extraordinary physics, the entire science of permafrost (itself a calque into English of the Russian *vechnaia merzlota*), semiconductor heterojunctions, hypergolic rocket fuels and so on.

But even broken clocks are right twice a day. Isn't our way of organizing science *best*, or at least better? After all, the Western system survived, even metastasized across the globe, and the Soviet system vanished with the empire that had spawned it. The question seems to me unanswerable. Metrics are defined within the context of a system. Americans won (many) more Nobel prizes than did Soviet citizens, but the Swedish Academy regularly snubbed the latter, and in any event usually could not read Russian to see what the fuss was about. There were fewer Soviet patents and inventions, but that's in no small part due to a radically different system of intellectual property, which preferred to compensate local geniuses with prizes and dachas. It doesn't seem to have been terribly *efficient*—an omnipresent critique of Soviet life in general—but I have seen few convincing measures of the efficiency of our own science system. (In any event, valorizing efficiency is an ideological criterion that characterizes our own science system—a forest of impact factors and performance metrics.)

To avert any misunderstanding: I am not *defending* the Soviet Science System; I am describing it. There was a great deal of shoddy work, rent-seeking and suffering within that system. But there was also extremely good *work*, and the latter was a product of the system that engendered the former. That's the paradox that comes from looking at any science system: it wouldn't be a system at all if it didn't, in some sense, work. The American system has its own pathologies—creationist brush-fires and politicized funding panels—many of them born of the relative openness of media and the potential for expert judgment (and funding) to be subject to the whims of demagogues, cranks and zealots. Those features seem pretty normal to us, but they struck Soviet citizens as destructive of the essence of science.

There is no escaping the stubborn reality that our expectations of scientific normalcy, our epistemic sensibilities, are hardwired into our science systems. These systems have evolved in order to organize expertise in accordance with those expectations. At the same time, science systems acquire emergent properties of their own which subtly shift those sensibilities. However extraordinary the phenomenon of Soviet science appears today, we cannot forget that for a significant segment of the world's scientists it was simply how science was done, just as our system manifests to our minds not as a science system, but simply *science*, full stop.

POPULAR SCIENCE

by Adam Alter

The first thing I learned in law school is that law school is not for learning the law. My decorated professor explained that we would spend twenty hours each week reading and discussing cases—and that very few of those cases would ever again figure in our lives as lawyers. Those hours were not wasted, but it was not because they filled our heads with legal content that they were useful. It was because they slowly formed us into the kinds of minds that make successful lawyers.

My professor was right. I began to speak, think and consume information like a lawyer. When I joined a large corporate law firm as a paralegal, I was coiled and ready to be lawyerly. Not a single one of the dozens of cases we discussed for thousands of hours appeared again, but that didn't matter. I was primed to read dozens of new cases quickly and efficiently, and to distill thousands of pages of judicial content into a rich concentrate of legal argument.

Eventually I left the law firm and embarked on a new life. I started and finished a doctorate in social psychology, began an academic job in psychology and marketing, and wrote a book. The book, written for people who are interested in human psychology but have no background in the subject, consumed me for three years. I wanted to share with other people the ideas that had kept my mind occupied and entertained for more than a decade. I created a document entitled "Book Plan" and filled page after page with references to my favorite experiments—first dozens and then hundreds. "Book Plan" became a catalogue of the content that populated my thoughts, the closest thing to a facsimile of my academic mind. My aim, I decided, should be to transfer as much of that information to the reader who happened to pick up my book.

I wrote intensely, but briefly. Tattooing my mind to the page wasn't working. My law professor had promised not to bombard us with content, but that's exactly what I was doing to my readers—giving them a brute-force education in social psychology. I stopped writing and spent some time leafing through popular-science classics. Some were written by academics in their respective fields, others by journalists and writers. The best of them presented ideas, but these ideas were mostly dressed in anecdotes and narratives.

The first book I opened when I prematurely stopped writing was Malcolm Gladwell's *The Tipping Point*. When I first read the book I was two years into a psychology degree, and it explains in no small part why I went on to pursue a Ph.D.—and why ten years later I wrote a book of my own. In this, his first book, Gladwell explores why some ideas, trends and products go viral after crossing the eponymous tipping point. What distinguishes this book from almost every other I had read before it is its complete disregard of intellectual boundaries. Gladwell is omnivorous, picking and choosing the most compelling ideas from more than a dozen fields. The references at the back of the book show traces of psychology, sociology, medicine, epidemiology, ethology, mathematics, marketing, history, public policy, communications theory, media studies, criminology, jurisprudence, evolutionary behavior, linguistics, public health and psychiatry. Gladwell is a wonderful writer and I enjoyed the book immensely, but long after my memories for each anecdote grew hazy—why crime rates in New York City fell in the mid-Nineties, why the cool kids suddenly started wearing Hush Puppies—I continued to see the world through a sharper lens. As a psychologist, I saw no reason why I couldn't dip my toes into thousands of other discipline-driven universes that fill our world with information.

A decade after reading *The Tipping Point*, I stumbled on a book called *The Secret Life of Pronouns*, written by psychologist James Pennebaker. Pennebaker and Gladwell are very different authors. Pennebaker writes about his own work, so his book covers a narrow field of information in great depth. But his book had a similarly profound impact on how I think about the world. Pennebaker's premise is that the "small, stealthy [function] words" we use every day—*you, a, am, to, I, but, the, for, not*—actually reveal a tremendous amount about our mental lives. He presents a string of compelling anecdotes and chases each one with empirical proof.

In one, he analyzes the correspondence between psychoanalysts Sigmund Freud and Carl Jung, who exchanged at least 337 letters between 1906 and 1913. Freud's reputation ascended before Jung's, but by 1911 both had achieved renown in the psychoanalytic community—and so the tension between them escalated. At first, their letters showed a great deal of linguistic mimicry; both scholars used similar function words, and their relationship flourished. By 1913, their views had diverged, and Freud suggested they "abandon ... personal relations entirely." Pennebaker shows that even before their letters grew hostile, their linguistic styles had begun to drift apart. These "small, stealthy words" betrayed animus long before it rose to the surface of their relationship.

What struck me about *The Secret Life of Pronouns*, and Pennebaker's research program more broadly, is that it achieves so many ends that are difficult to accomplish simultaneously. Pennebaker shows that large effects grow from small, apparently innocuous roots, and that those effects persist across many domains, from presidential speeches and letters between academics to Shakespearean character arcs and Beatles lyrics. In each case, function words predict vast differences in power, affection, self-deception, success and leadership skills. As with Gladwell's book, long after the details from Pennebaker's anecdotes have begun to fade, I find myself reading legal and political transcripts differently, listening to how other people speak differently, and understanding the world differently.

Gladwell's book succeeded because it eradicated the barriers between disciplines; Pennebaker's succeeded because it presented one very powerful idea that tied together disparate worlds. But neither book succeeded because it filled my mind with content. The case studies made the books fun to read, but over time my memory for them waned and left behind a sketchy trace of the big ideas that made the books enduringly important. The vivid anecdotes were just the vehicles that transported those big ideas.

To me, then, the essence of good science writing is not the sharing of particular ideas, but the sharing of general approaches to perceiving the world. A book doesn't succeed because its readers can cite ten new facts; it succeeds because the next time those readers see a person behaving oddly, or the sun at a particular height in the sky, or two birds engaged in an elaborate courtship ritual, they look at those events differently and perhaps more deeply. This is a skill that cuts across every sphere of life and promises to bring great rewards across time.

Both Gladwell and Pennebaker change how we look at the world, but Gladwell's lesson is broader than Pennebaker's. Gladwell implies that the most interesting way to look at the world is to develop a voracious appetite for information without paying too much attention to which discipline produced that information. When several disciplines tackle big challenges—crime, poverty, education, prejudice, disease—it makes no sense to doggedly rely on one approach without at least considering the others. This might seem obvious, but expertise—burrowing deeply into one subject—often comes at the expense of breadth. The first chapter of *The Tipping Point* illustrates Gladwell's approach perfectly. As he sketches the "three rules of epidemics," he invokes lessons from epidemiologists (who were investigating a syphilis epidemic in Baltimore); businesspeople (who were trying to repeat the success of Hush Puppies, which went from selling 30,000 pairs of shoes per year in the early 1990s to 430,000 pairs in 1995); and psychologists (who wondered why dozens of bystanders chose not to intervene or call for help as a young woman was brutally attacked). There are conferences for epidemiologists, conferences for businesspeople and conferences for psychologists—but none that encourage all three disciplines to come together as seamlessly as they do in Gladwell's book.

Pennebaker's lesson is narrower but no less important. He shows how a specific, obscure idea at the avant-garde of his field illuminates new terrain for anyone who's willing to learn. This is a valuable service, particularly in aggregate, as academics who write similar books incrementally bridge the chasm between academia and everything else. It's easiest to see how important this process is by focusing on how much the chasm shrank during the twentieth century. Concepts that were restricted to experts are understood far more widely today: the forces of supply and demand from economics; sterilization and infection from medicine; the relationship between natural light and well-being from psychology. String together enough of these ideas, and the average well-read layperson becomes the sum of a diverse range of experts—shallower and less sophisticated than true experts, of course, but a smarter consumer of the world's information nonetheless.

Psychologists use the term *metacognition* to label how we think about our thoughts, and a truly great popular science book changes how we approach the business of thinking, rather than the specific things we think about. My law professor was explaining this idea without the jargon—that law school changes how you approach the task of consuming information—and books like *The Tipping Point* and *The Secret Life of Pronouns* achieve the same lofty goal. Once you've read them, you perceive the same people, places, objects, ideas and concepts through a more sophisticated lens. Nothing looks the same, because you're sporting an upgrade in your basic mental apparatus.

AN INTERVIEW WITH MICHAEL LEMONICK

MICHAEL LEMONICK IS a science journalist who has spent the last several years focusing on climate change, writing over fifty cover stories for *Time* magazine as well as six books, the most recent of which is *Mirror Earth: The Search for Our Planet's Twin* (2012). He is currently a writer-at-large for Climate Central, an independent organization of scientists and journalists that researches and reports on climate change and its consequences. A few weeks before the Intergovernmental Panel on Climate Change (IPCC) published the second part of its landmark Fifth Assessment report, *The Point* had a chance to ask Lemonick how journalists can tell compelling but accurate stories about climate change in an era when Google thinks people are more likely to search "climate change hoax" than "climate change effects."

•

The Point: *So tell us about Climate Central.*

Michael Lemonick: The ambition of Climate Central is to make climate change something that people think about and take seriously. We do climate journalism but we also do some basic climate research—not quite science, more like data mining and processing to put climate information into a context that people understand, with the hope that other news organizations will pick up and discuss the reports we issue. We also try to convince TV meteorologists to use our graphics and to talk about climate change in their weather reports.

The Point: *Do you think that Climate Central's structure could be incorporated into a normal news organization, such that on their science stories they have both a journalist and a scientist?*

ML: I think it would be very difficult. It would be very difficult because, whereas a public television station or a nonprofit company like Climate Central doesn't have to earn money and is not really competing in a financial sense with other media outlets, if you go to a real newspaper or TV station, while they would like to have accurate stories, what they *must* have are stories that beat the competition and raise their profile. And they need to be able to do things fast. The idea of writing a story for a magazine and saying, "OK, well, now we'll go to the scientists and negotiate back and forth for several hours"... If I said that to an editor, he or she would look at me as though I'd lost my mind.

The Point: *But let's say you had unlimited time to do a story, would there still be a problem? Would the accuracy—the total accuracy—demanded by a scientist be a problem?*

ML: Yes, it could be a problem because the only way that a story in a newspaper or a magazine could legitimately be considered completely accurate would be for you to reprint the relevant scientific paper in its entirety. Anything that you do that changes the paper in any way, that leaves anything out, already starts to make it false at some level. But since no ordinary person would ever want to read a scientific paper, you

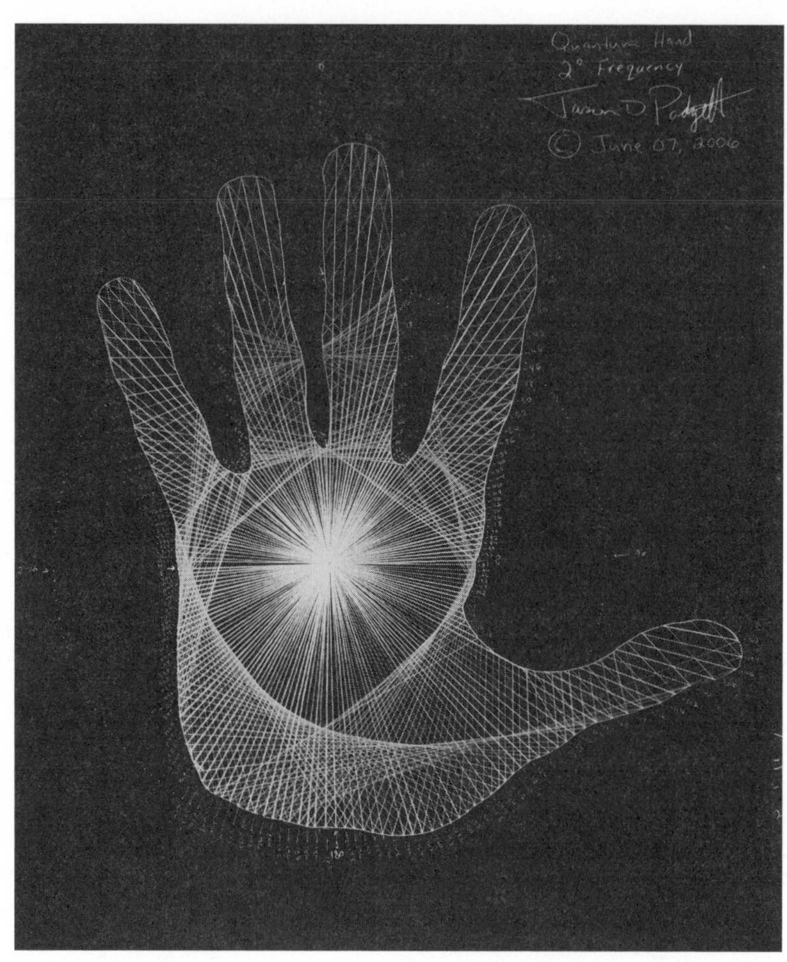

Jason Padgett, *Quantum Hand*, 2006

can't be accurate to that degree. After that, it's all a question of compromises, how precise you have to be and how many references and charts and methods you need to have.

The Point: *Has the institution as a whole succeeded given its original end?*

ML: I don't know for certain that it has raised the public's awareness about climate. My theory is that nothing that any journalist or scientist has done since I started writing about this topic in 1987 has *significantly* raised the public consciousness about climate change. Al Gore did with the movie in 2006, briefly, but basically nothing has worked—except for the natural world having given us a few years of very clearly extreme weather, which may or may not be attributable to climate change but which has people thinking about climate change and has them open to reading stories about climate change. It's something that we're now taking advantage of. The profile of the organization is higher and people in the organization have higher profiles as a result. We had our lead writer poached by another website and there was a story on one of the journalism review sites or somewhere, maybe it was on Gawker, which talked about the fact that all of a sudden having a climate-slash-weather journalist on your payroll is really important. And it's not because the quality of climate journalism has suddenly gotten really good. It's that people are suddenly interested, for reasons that might or might not be specious.

The Point: *Does that worry you? Is there a conflation of climate and weather?*

ML: It worries me to a degree. I mean, the question is obviously: Is it OK to gloss over the difference between climate and weather if that results in more people being aware about climate change? Ethically, probably not entirely. But does it matter? It disserves me but I'm not sure I would rail against it, if you see what I mean.

The Point: *Why do you think it has been so hard for people to absorb the information about climate change? I was taught about climate change and global warming when I was maybe nine or ten, at school. At the same time it was taught in Germany and they just went and did stuff about it. You see wind farms all over and if you go to a city like Freiburg, much of the energy is now renewable. They just acted on it. Why is it that we in the U.S. and the U.K. have been much slower to even believe it, or to act on it?*

ML: Local culture, I think that's what it is. The idea that making sacrifices for the collective good is antithetical to American values. You know, "We went out on the frontier and conquered the continent and killed off the people who lived there and we're self-reliant and built our own log cabins…" That's part of the American identity: individual liberties, don't tell me what to do, keep the government out of my business. I think that's a big part of it.

The Point: *Do you think it will ever change?*

ML: That is a sociological question that I am unqualified to answer. Let me put it this way, however: When I was growing up in the 1960s there was a sense that it was changing in a big way. In the Thirties, the government had instituted Social Security and in the Sixties the government instituted the Medicare program and the EPA was founded to help protect us against pollution and environmental harm. So there was a sense that the culture was moving in a direction of greater appreciation for the collective good and for the rights of minorities of various kinds. And we now look fifty years later and that's proved to be largely a sham, a veneer placed over these basic assumptions that haven't really changed at all.

The Point: *Maybe the current situation is even worse than you're suggesting. In the Sixties the question was how we could come together for the collective good, where the collective good was basically American. Whereas now it's the global collective and so Americans have to act not only for the good of the country but for the good of the world. And it might be the case, might it not, that Americans wouldn't suffer from climate change as much as people elsewhere?*

ML: Certainly not as much as people from countries with a lot fewer resources. So yes, I think that's absolutely right. It's also true that climate change is remote in time. There are many things I have to worry about more immediate than whether my furnace is highly efficient, so it feels like something remote. That's why extreme weather has made people stop and think, "It's not so remote. I lost power for a week in Hurricane Sandy." All we can do is allow extreme weather events to continue happening and allow people to keep reacting to them in dismay, until they're so beaten up by economic losses from the drought in California or whatever—

The Point: *Then it's your job to stand back and let misinformation perpetuate.*

ML: What misinformation?

The Point: *That extreme weather…*

ML: Well, one extreme storm means nothing; one drought means nothing. But if over ten years eight of them are drought years, that starts to mean something. If over 30 years, 28 of them are drought years, that really starts to mean something.

The Point: *Well how much time do we have? Perhaps we don't have thirty years to prove the point.*

ML: We may or may not have time to wait, but the public consciousness is not obliged to what your sense of what there's time for. I remember when, in 1964, the Surgeon General of the U.S. declared that smoking causes cancer—and smoking does cause cancer, no question about it. It's similar to climate in that whether you do something today or tomorrow really means nothing; it has to be over the long term. If in 1964 some politician had stood up and said, "I'm ordering that smoking be banned in all federal buildings, and in restaurants, and on airplanes, and on trains, and if you want to smoke in an office building you need to go huddle outside in the driving rain like a pariah"—if you'd said all those things in 1964, people would have thought you were crazy. People would have been outraged, despite the fact that this had been objectively shown to be true. It took many, many years.

The Point: *And what accounted for that long-term change in consciousness?*

ML: I don't know exactly what it was, but I think it had to do with the fact that it was undeniable. The science was much clearer to people than the science of climate change is. Another difference is that action on climate change does seem to involve what appears to be economic sacrifice in the short run. If we require that all cars be efficient, how are we going to compete with countries that don't have those rules?

The Point: *I just want to push you a little bit about extreme weather. I'm not a scientist by any means, but I guess intuitively it makes sense to me why droughts might be on the increase with global warming. It doesn't make sense to me why hurricanes should be.*

ML: Well, I'll tell you why they should. The reason they should is that hurricanes get their energy from the heat in seawater. And so the higher the sea surface temperature the more energy is available to turn a tropical depression into a tropical storm and turn a tropical storm into a hurricane. So that's the reasoning. And that's why in 2005 people were saying we should expect hurricanes to increase. More research, more looking at historical records and so on, caused a modification of that idea, because it turns out that sea surface temperature is not the only factor in making hurricanes. Another is atmospheric wind shear. The conventional wisdom now, although it is not completely accepted, is that hurricanes are likely to become less frequent, but when they do form they'll be more powerful.

The Point: *That kind of case will be hard to translate into action on climate change.*

ML: But ordinary people make that connection anyway: "Climate change is gonna make the weather crazy, and look, the weather's crazy!"

The Point: *People also make it in the bad way. "Have you noticed how cold it's been in Chicago? Global warming, whatever."*

ML: They can try to do that. We're there to show them a map of the world during this winter that shows the entire world in red, and then this little piece of the U.S. in blue. It's not a perfect system that I'm talking about, but I think that if you don't work too strenuously to discourage people from drawing conclusions that aren't valid, but are in your favor, and you do work very hard to discourage them from drawing false conclusions that are not in your favor...

The Point: *So is there a danger of falling into the kind of trap that caused the East Anglia scandal, where emails seemed to reveal that researchers were a little too politically committed? What's your view on what happened there?*

ML: Well, I think that people who are actively hostile to climate science harassed that East Anglia group mercilessly, and the researchers responded by emailing each other, saying, "I wish I could beat these people up," as any normal human would do. And then when that stuff was revealed, the perpetrators could be indignant: "I'm shocked that people would talk about us this way; it shows us how bankrupt the whole system is." I thought it was completely sleazy.

The Point: *But you must agree there's a general possibility of thinking that one should deceive for the sake of the truth. We do it often, with children for example, and one could imagine a doctor doing it: "This won't hurt, don't worry."*

ML: So what does it mean to deceive? Does it mean to actively say things that are not true?

The Point: *Or just being economical with the truth. It does seem like that is implicitly happening. You've pointed out the rise of the weather*

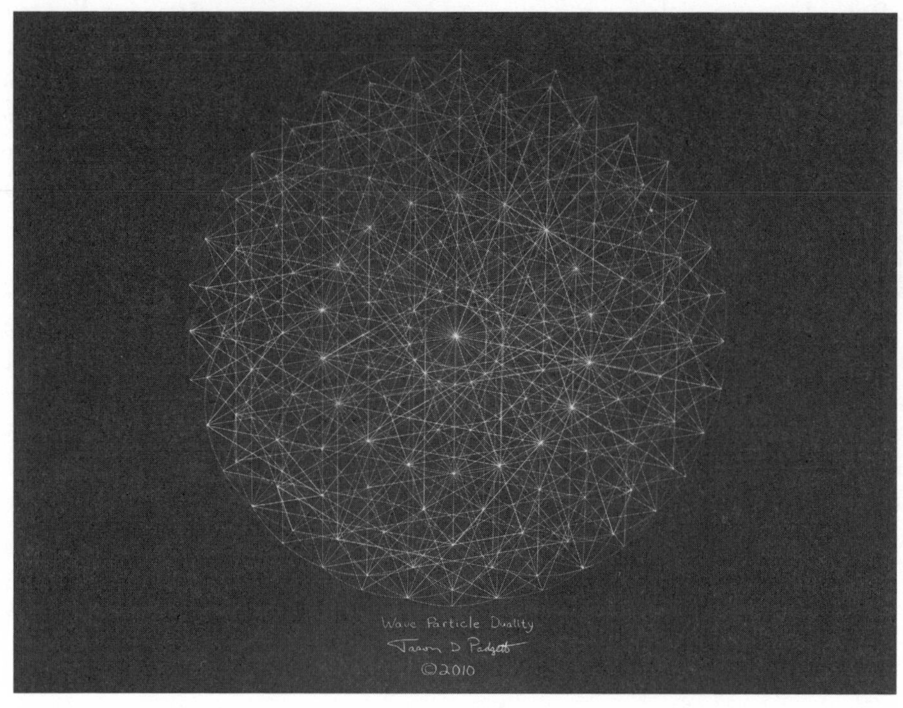

Jason Padgett, *Wave Particle Duality*, 2010

nerds and how climate stories are becoming more and more desirable to report. But it wouldn't be a news story to say this year has actually been quite mild. It might be one news story, but it wouldn't be a news splash. There's not a story in the way Hurricane Sandy is a story.

ML: Right, and I think that there is a danger in hitching your wagon to some of these stories. Because if next winter is just a perfectly average winter, people who are trying to cast doubt on climate science might well say, "See, you guys were talking about how it's getting warmer."

The Point: *Even when the news is in your favor, you should still emphasize that even if it hadn't happened, we would still, roughly speaking, be in the same position about climate change.*

ML: And we do talk about that. People talk about the pause in global warming after 1998. When I write a story about it, I talk very openly about the fact that some people claim there is evidence that global warming has stopped. But 2000-2010 was the warmest decade on record and the long-term trend over the twentieth century is clear. There are other places where it has slowed down, but overall the trend has always been upward. It's not surprising that natural climate variation would have an effect when superimposed on human-induced climate variation. Sometimes the combination would accelerate warming; sometimes it would slow it down. These sort of slowdowns show up in climate models, contrary to what people assume. It's not that the models fail to predict—they may have failed to predict this particular incident at this particular time, but they predict such things all the time. So the argument that global warming has stopped is not something to be taken seriously.

The Point: *Do you think that the public just has a problem with probabilistic reasoning?*

ML: Oh yeah. Absolutely. It is hard to grasp.

The Point: *People say that with medical stories in particular, the uptake of statistical information is extraordinarily poor.*

ML: That's right. And yet journalists want to tell a good story. If some study shows some disease can be cured in a mouse, the reality is that it probably will not lead to a human cure. So if I started my story by saying, "In a development that is most likely going to have no effect on human health whatever, scientists announce today that they have done such and such," nobody would read past that sentence. If I said, "In a development that *could* someday lead to a human cure," which is technically true, they'll keep reading. Another problem with medical stories is that statistics about changes in prognosis are often expressed in relative risk. If you eat more cheese, you are *twice* as likely to get a heart attack. But if you have a one percent chance beforehand, now you're at 2 percent, so you're still 98 percent certain you won't have a heart attack. We often put things in terms of relative risk because it seems more significant. It's a better story.

The Point: *Suppose the world just got colder in the next twenty years, it seems fair to say that that wouldn't actually disprove the current theories, in that those theories are probabilistic and therefore do allow a very small probability that things will go the other way.*

ML: The theory comes in several levels. First, we're putting more carbon dioxide in the atmosphere. That could be falsified if we measured it and we weren't, but we have measured it and we are. Second, that all other things being equal, that will tend to warm the planet. But all other things are not equal. And so an outside natural change, such as a change in the brightness of the sun, could overwhelm the effect from human emissions. Another point is that there are many feedback mechanisms in the climate system, some of which could speed things up, some of which could slow things down. Thirty years ago, it was much less clear how those would play out. Now it looks as though the feedbacks that make the climate warm even faster are more robustly understood than the feedbacks that cool it off. That's where the 99 percent comes in, but it's only that part of the theory that would be falsified anyway, not the basic premise.

The Point: *A big topic nowadays is how we use science in political debate. What's your general assessment of that?*

ML: See, the problem is that politics is carried out by politicians. And politicians do not have a strong incentive to tell the truth. They have a strong incentive to avoid the truth because it might get somebody annoyed. I consider politicians a necessary evil. Somebody called me about political ads during some election and my response was, "I consider all political ads to be a blanket of lies wrapped around a kernel of truth." I am very cynical about politics and I don't have anything constructive to say. I don't think highly enough of politicians to think that they will ever get it together in this country.

The Point: *Now, do you think that's a problem which journalism could theoretically ameliorate, in that if you educate the public enough, then politicians will simply not be able to make this kind of—*

ML: [*Incredulously*] What planet do you live on? I don't believe that for a minute. I don't think the public wants to be educated. The public is interested in reinforcing their own preexisting beliefs.

The Point: *But theoretically—*

ML: Well, oh, theoretically, yes.

The Point: *But even beyond theoretically, it's an information-purveying—*

ML: Yeah, well, was it H. L. Mencken who said, "No one ever went broke underestimating the intelligence of the American public"?

The Point: *Yeah, Mencken. You say you despise politicians. In a way, you sound like you wish there weren't—*

ML: Oh, I don't have any better solution, if that's what you're going to ask me.

The Point: *Well it sounds a bit like you have a technocratic—*

ML: Oh! Benevolent dictatorship. Sure! Let me be the dictator and everything will be fine.

The Point: *Or rule by experts. Isn't that the approach Obama is taking by saying, "We can't get Congress to pass any laws regarding climate change, so what I'm going to do is go directly to*

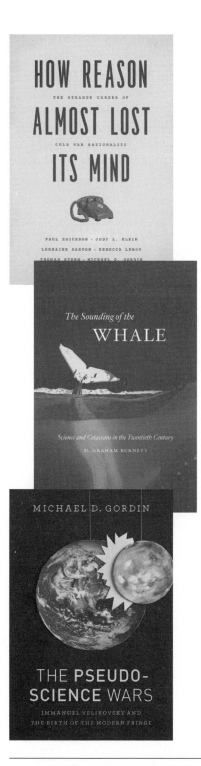

the EPA and impose regulations"? What do you make of that strategy? Is that also a necessary evil?

ML: See, I like that strategy. I think climate change is serious, so I favor many of the policies he advocates and I am more than happy for him to do what he needs to get around the intransigence of his opposition.

The Point: *In Max Weber you have the idea that there's a real problem when experts get in the way of politics because politics is the realm of setting ends, and expertise can only tell us about means. It can tell us about the facts, and it can tell us how we can get somewhere, should we want to go. What science cannot do is tell us where we want to go. It seems to me that on the Left in the U.S., with respect to climate change, there is just a thought that we'll leave it up to the scientists rather than making normative arguments ourselves.*

ML: But do we really leave it up to the scientists to say what path we should follow? There are people on the Left who are vehemently against nuclear power and then there are people who say we must have nuclear power because of climate change. So I endorse the thought that we should leave it to the experts to tell us what the facts are about the case, leave it to the experts to tell us what the most effective ways are of achieving goals, and then we'll decide what to do.

The Point: *Now what would you say if someone said, "OK, taking into account all the facts, I don't think we should do anything about climate change"?*

ML: Well, that is, in fact, pretty much the situation. And I think it's extremely frustrating.

The Point: *But isn't that a possible reasonable position? The argument would be that we should spend our money on other things.*

ML: It is possible. I mean, to take it to an extreme, if I'm a Jehovah's Witness and I'm told, "You must have a blood transfusion or you will die tomorrow," I don't think it's *reasonable* to say, "It's against my beliefs so I won't take the transfusion," but I do think it is my *right* to do that. Of course, that just involves one person.

The Point: *But hasn't it become fairly normal to demonize someone who makes that argument? Imagine someone who said, "Yeah, there is climate change, but, given the various difficulties of acting on it—we don't have a world government, that kind of thing—we're never going to be able to change this, so let's try to find some ways of ameliorating the effects." Someone who said that, I think, would be demonized. It's out of the mainstream.*

ML: But they would be less demonized than somebody who says it is not happening at all. There's a guy in Denmark, Bjørn Lomborg, who does take that approach and he is demonized by a lot of... maybe leftists, maybe not, but certainly a lot of climate scientists. I've never quite understood why he upsets them so much.

The Point: *I was actually thinking about him in particular. I saw him talk in maybe 2003 and he was just reviled for his views. Really what he was claiming was just that although climate change is indeed happening, "I've done some cost-benefit analyses and it's not that it is not a real problem, nor is it that we couldn't do anything about it, but given the costs of doing something about it, we'd be better off spending that money doing something* *like, say, building wells in Africa. If you're worried about the effect of climate change on Africans because it will make a difference on their day-to-day lives, well, what would make a much bigger difference is having drinking water. An extra one or two degrees isn't going to matter to them as much as drinking water, lack of productive agriculture and so on, so that's where we should be spending our money." And he was vilified.*

ML: I think there's certainly a resistance in many quarters to acknowledging (a) that there might be better ways to spend our money and (b) that we should begin to figure out how to adapt to climate change, because people think that takes away from the public's concern to prevent it.

The Point: *This ties into some of what we were talking about earlier in the sense of being economical with the truth and trying to shape people. The best-case scenario is that everyone's opinions change such that climate change doesn't happen because we make changes to our way of life so that it doesn't happen. The next best scenario is that climate change happens and we're prepared for it. The worst-case scenario is that climate change happens and we're not prepared for it. And there's a danger that in aiming for number one we might end up at number three.*

ML: I think that's already changing, though: I think climate scientists and climate advocacy groups are much more willing to talk about adaptation than they used to be. The IPCC issued a short interim report in maybe 2011 that talked about adaptation, that talked about resiliency of communities, that talked about the fact that the impact of climate depends not just on what the climate does in and of itself but also on what the local infrastructure is and so on.

The Point: *Why do you think the Right isn't more willing to make that kind of case about climate change? What is it about denying? I mean, it seems to be a very American thing, this denial of the truth of climate change. I think it's fair to say that in the U.K. it would be more of this Lomborg-type argument, e.g. "Yes, we admit that this is happening but we can't sacrifice good British jobs," but here you deny the premise.*

ML: Well, these scientists that are deniers would get no attention at all if it weren't that it played into a political agenda on the Right, where people come from districts where the idea of government mandates is rejected outright.

The Point: *It's not just the Right. It's important to point out that John Dingell, for example—who's just retiring as a Democratic congressman for the Detroit suburbs—is extremely against this. The same with the West Virginia senators, who are both Democrats. There's this very close tie to your district's economic interests. So it's too simple to say it's the Right. But the basic point is that in America people who don't want us to act on climate change are more willing to insist it's just not happening. Do they really believe that it's not happening?*

ML: Well, it's what I was saying before: they will avoid the truth if it hurts them politically.

The Point: *So they too could make the case that they are being economical with the truth for the sake of the truth. That people couldn't handle it. Were I to make the complex argument that there is climate change but there's nothing we can do about it—people can't handle that, so I just won't tell them.*

ML: It's not that the people can't handle it; it's just that the politician's opponents

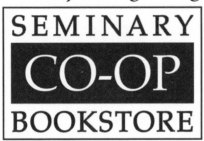

would beat him over the head and he would be turned out in the next primary for wavering from absolute rejection of climate change. There's also this mistrust of authority more generally, a mistrust of experts, a mistrust of scientists.

The Point: *This brings us to the question of the institutions of journalism, the practice of journalism in the United States. Because when you say that these climate change deniers wouldn't get a hearing elsewhere, I think there's some truth in that. It strikes me that the notion of objectivity at work in American journalism, the notion of being fair and balanced, is that wherever a question is considered to be controversial at all you should have one view on one side, and one view on the other. Whereas in science it's not the case that every argument has two equally weighted sides. There's the extremely marginal weirdo and then there's the dominant view. And the American approach gives a voice at the table to the marginal person. Would you agree with that?*

ML: I would. And that's something that journalists have been thinking about for a while and that scientists have been complaining about for a while. But most major news outlets don't do it anymore. I think it comes from political journalism, where it's much harder to figure out who's right and who's wrong, and you have to let both sides speak.

reviews

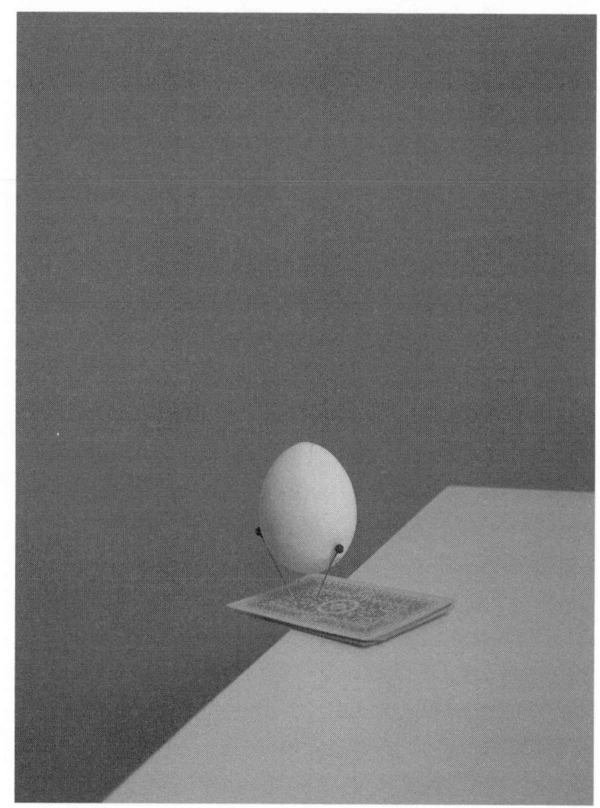

Csilla Klenyánszki, *Eggs on Pins*, 2013

NOMA

by Jacob Mikanowski

May you grow like an onion, with your head in the ground.

Old Yiddish Curse

THIS IS HOW you cook potatoes the Noma way: Find an organic farm in the Danish countryside. Persuade the farmer to leave a field fallow for a full year and then have him dry out the hundreds of kinds of grasses, plant tops and weeds that have grown in it in the absence of crops. Unearth a few new potatoes fresh from a neighboring field. Pack each one individually in the dried weeds. Then wrap them in salt dough. Roast. When they're done, mash them lightly with a little bit of butter. Pack the mash in skins made of dehydrated milk, creating "ravioli." Sprinkle with wild herbs, chickweed, yarrow and glazed snails. Add a sauce of buttermilk blended with newly cut grass. Prepared this way, the dish should allow the green flavors from one field to merge with those of the potatoes from below. According to René Redzepi, the chef who created it, the completed ensemble should taste "exactly like the wonderful, heartwarming scent of a freshly mowed lawn on a summer's day."

When Redzepi described this recipe in front of a packed audience at San Francisco's Castro Theatre this past November, I found myself strangely moved. It sounds like a lot of work, but it contains a beautiful thought, of hay, herbs, sun, grass, earth, a particular season in a particular place. It's like something out of a poem by Wordsworth or John Clare. It's the kind of recipe that has lifted Redzepi to culinary fame. In the nine years since he opened his restaurant in a Copenhagen warehouse, Noma (the name is a combination of the Danish words for Nordic and food) has become one of the most sought-after tables in the world. Starting in 2010, it was named the best restaurant in the world three years in a row, a position it only lost this year, to El Celler de Can Roca in Spain.

Given these accolades, it's perhaps no surprise that Redzepi could draw a crowd of over a thousand to a lecture and cookbook signing, or that he was introduced by his fellow Dane, Metallica drummer Lars Ulrich, as an artistic genius on par with Picasso and Pollock. (Ulrich collects art.) Still, I couldn't help wondering what we were all doing there. After all, only a handful of people in the audience had ever eaten at Noma, and chances are only a handful ever will. Redzepi himself seemed a little shocked by the attention. As he writes in the journal that accompanies his new book of recipes, "No one cared what a chef had to say" in the past. "When did restaurant chefs leave the kitchen ... to get projected into this?" he asked from the stage, before launching into stories about his decision to serve live ants to his customers (they taste like lemongrass) and his lengthy quest to make a worthwhile dish out of lamb brains.

IT TURNS OUT that the trick with the lamb brains is to treat them as a spread and an accompaniment to bread. They have a difficult texture—"in between foie gras and fish sperm"—and you can't overcook them (they fall apart) or let them dry out (the results are apparently too horrifying for words). The solution to Redzepi's other question, of when chefs started to occupy a central position in the culture, is a bit harder to pinpoint. Though in San Francisco, at least, the answer is: some time ago. And not just because this is a city where no matter what else is going on—skyrocketing rents, police shootings, municipal corruption—the people you meet always want to tell you about their newest breakthrough with food.

The Bay Area is America's incubator of utopias. And for the past forty years, one of the principal ways these utopias have articulated their vision of the world is through food. From the hippie communes of the Sixties and Seventies to the techno-futurist bubble cities of today, each utopia has developed a cuisine of its own and, usually, an ideology to go with it. But while in the past this often had to do with negotiating human relationships to nature, now it has more to do with technology. We've gone from back-to-the-land-ism and organic farming to software and engineering, with tech moguls and hackers testing the limits of food's perfectibility.

Another way of saying this is that, in the Bay Area, an extraordinary number of millionaire geniuses spend prodigious amounts of money in pursuit of the perfect burger or cup of coffee. Jack Dorsey, the co-creator of Twitter, owns Sightglass, a South-of-Market coffee shop that used the latest in imported

Japanese technology—halogen siphons—to make superior espressos before they switched to something even fancier. On Valencia in the Mission, two young tech multimillionaires have plowed their earnings into a tailor-made urban chocolate factory that crafts elegant (and expensive) bars from beans sourced from individual farms in Ecuador and Madagascar. Then there's the recent Columbia graduate who almost started his own version of Facebook while in college. Even though his company didn't go anywhere, he made a fortune and now roams the earth dining at the best restaurants and posting endless reviews and Instagram photos on his blog, which reads like a modern-day update of John Cheever's *Swimmer*.

Of all the technologists trying to remake themselves in the food world, perhaps none have gone further than Nathan Myhrvold. The longtime head of technology at Microsoft, and now the head of a predatory multibillion-dollar patent farm, Myhrvold has devoted years—and millions of dollars—to remaking cooking along rational, scientific lines. The fruit of his labor is a five-volume, ten-pound book called *Modernist Cuisine*, in which hundreds of kitchen staples are reimagined as baroque marvels of techno-futurist cookery. They're very hard to make. Take his burger, in which every component—including the bun and ketchup—is made from scratch, and whose ingredients are meticulously tweaked to achieve the laboratory-tested optimum flavor profile: The lettuce is infused sous-vide with hickory smoke, the cheese is aged in wheat ale, the tomato is vacuum-compressed, and the whole thing is covered in a glaze of suet, tomato confit, beef stock and smoked fat. The patty itself gets cooked sous-vide in suet, dropped in a liquid nitrogen bath, and deep fried.

However intense its flavors, the burger takes hundreds of combined man-hours to make and requires equipment not normally found in all but the most elite restaurant kitchens. Myhrvold's work conjures a world in which comfort food is made with the same precision engineering and allowance for luxury that goes into the construction of rich-guy yachts and custom jets. It's a perfect expression of his whole mode of life as amateur paleontologist, corporate raider, safari enthusiast, patent troll, eighties Bond villain and Willy Wonka.

Yet the scale of Myhrvold's ambition pales beside that animating the makers of a new food substitute named Soylent, after the fictional food infamously made from dead humans in the 1973 film *Soylent Green*. A high-energy mix of nutritive powders—oat flour, tapioca maltodextrin, rice-protein powder and canola oil—boosted with a number of vitamins, minerals and other additives, Soylent has a "sour, wheaty" taste and, when combined with water, a texture like diluted oatmeal. But flavor isn't the point. Soylent was developed by a young computer programmer named Rob Rhinehart who was frustrated with his body's need to consume food three times a day. Soylent was his solution. It is supposed to contain all the vitamins, proteins, amino acids and sugars needed to sustain the body—indefinitely.

According to most who have tried it, Soylent is a bland, if not nauseating, gruel. It is non-food. But it carries with it a revolutionary potential: to liberate the mind from the tyranny of the body. It promises to be the last meal you ever have to eat (or drink). Soylent has proved to be remarkably popular, raising $100,000 in pre-orders in only a few hours online and eventually winning over $1.5 million in venture-capital funding. It seems especially popular with people interested in hacking their biology as if it were another piece of hardware. I recently overheard a young computer programmer say that he had purchased a week's supply as an experiment. Talking to *New York Magazine*, Zach Alexander, a 30-year-old software developer and an early adopter of Soylent, explained its appeal like this: "For me cooking is like an art form. And it's really frustrating how biology compels you to eat food three times a day even though you don't want to."

The same kind of scientific tinkering that went into the design of Soylent has extended into the upper reaches of haute cuisine. In new modes of cooking, food gets dematerialized, turned into distilled scents and pure flavors. You can ingest whole meals with an eyedropper or a straw. It's almost abstract, and indeed the move in haute cuisine of the past decade or so has been a modernist one: to try to liberate what we eat from its connection to its origins. More and more, chefs have been trying to make food that doesn't taste or look or otherwise resemble the ingredients it is made out of.

In this, they've been led by Ferran Adrià, the Catalan chef in charge of the recently shuttered elBulli, probably the most influential restaurant of the new millennium. Using techniques drawn from the worlds of chemistry, physics and materials science, Adrià invented a host of ways to distill properties from one ingredient and infuse them into another. His cooking uses centrifuges, atomizers and industrial coolants. With them, he infuses scents into sprays, makes oils and liquids into gels, and turns semisolids like cheese or chocolate into unrecognizable landscapes. When the art critic Jerry Saltz ate at elBulli, he said that "nothing looked like what it was; nothing tasted like what it looked like."

In Adrià's "molecular gastronomy" (a term he hates, but which has stuck), flavor, smell, color and texture all act as independent variables, and can be recombined at will. With Adrià, dining is surrealism: caviar tastes like melon juice; olive oil arrives in the shape of a loop of wire or a gelatinous "olive"; a volleyball of frozen ice cream tastes like gorgonzola; popcorn balloons disappear when you touch them. Adrià's innovations have spread out across the food world over the years. It's now not uncommon to find foams and gels on menus

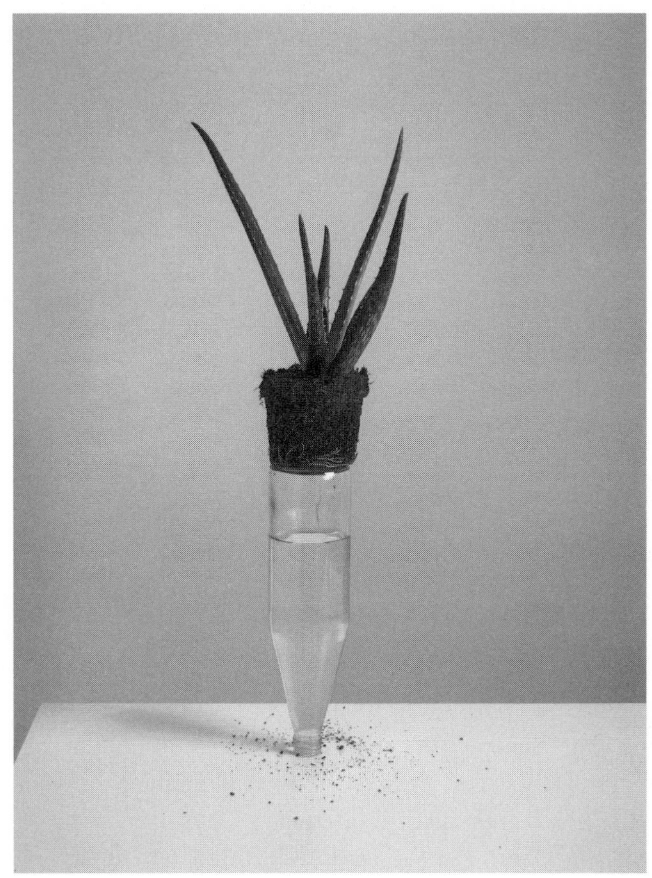

Csilla Klenyánszki, *Plant on Bottle*, 2013

in fancy restaurants and unconventional thermodynamics deployed in neighborhood bakeries. One of my favorite examples of the new scientific cuisine comes from a "contemporary patisserie" in San Francisco called Craftsmen and Wolves. They sell a ($7) savory muffin called the "Rebel Within." When you cut it open there's a perfectly cooked soft-boiled egg inside. How did it get there? Why didn't it set with the rest of the dough? I spent weeks trying to figure it out before someone told me the answer. (They supercool the egg in liquid nitrogen before they put it in the dough.) Knowing how it's done removes some of the initial satisfaction, but that mysterious molten egg still seems to me to embody what the technological approach to cooking can do at its best. It's a moment of domestic magic. That the ingenuity that goes into it so outstrips the result is essential to its charm; the pleasure lies in the conquest of the useless.

SO WHERE DOES René Redzepi fit in this new world of food? The nature-worshipping forager cuisine he's perfected at Noma seems at odds with both Ferran Adrià's scientific whimsy and Soylent's austere post-humanism. In actual fact, Redzepi apprenticed for a long time with Adrià, but his cooking doesn't feature many of his master's characteristic flourishes. Which is not to say he didn't learn anything from his time at elBulli: he uses gels and centrifuges, and engages in some elaborate deceptions, like making "twigs" out of deep-fried crisp bread coated with edible "lichens." But these advanced techniques aren't at the heart of his aesthetic. Rather, Redzepi's focus is on ingredients and on dishes that evoke the sense of a certain place and time.

This insight—"the plate should reflect the where and when of the guest"—came about gradually. At first, Noma was a fairly standard haute cuisine restaurant, making classic dishes with a few substitutions to give them a local flavor—for instance by using sour apple wine to make stock or sea buckthorn in place of vanilla for a crème brûlée. This went on for a while, until Redzepi, stuck in Greenland after a hunting trip, had a breakthrough: he realized that by relying on wild ingredients foraged from the Nordic countryside he could create something new—cooking that, according to him, speaks to a "truly personal and inspiring relationship to nature." From then on, his cooks took to scouring Danish beaches for aromatic sea grasses, searching hayfields for edible blossoms and interrogating farmers about individual batches of unripe strawberries. Soon thereafter, they started importing 200-year-old mahogany clams from Norway and edible lichens and mosses from the Swedish woods. Whole new categories of foodstuff came to their attention. The forest, especially, became Noma's larder. In his *Journal* (one part of his new three-book collection *René Redzepi: A Work in Progress*) Redzepi explains that, although often overlooked, trees offer so much: "There are the tiny shoots, the needles, the delicious sap, the gelatinous layer between the bark and the tree, the mosses and not to forget the fruit: the chestnuts, hazelnuts and so on."

The primal scenes of his creativity take place in the forest or on the beach. In the *Journal*, he remembers finding sea arrowgrass for the first time on a beach and being amazed at its bright, herbal flavor: "The juices burst into my mouth, salty like sea water and then an explosion of flavor, like the finale of a fireworks display: coriander ... From that day on the world looked different." Time and again he returns to the woods in search of inspiration:

> I went foraging, sinking into the forest, tasting things, hoping to clear my thoughts and take that deep, relaxing breath that allows me to shrug off the bustle of the kitchen. I took a second and rested on my haunches, absentmindedly picking things up around me. A snail slowly wandered through the moss. I followed as it inched along, unaware that it was selecting its own garnish. Back in the kitchen, the snail was cooked very tenderly, glazed a little in a tasty, intense broth, then lovingly encircled by cooked and raw roots, plants, shoots and flowers: it was a small mouthful representing a few square meters of a particular Danish forest on that exact day. It felt so satisfying to use my intuition in that way.

He's right—there is something alluring about all this: the silence of the forest, the coolness of the moss, the snail selecting its own garnish. But I don't think it's because of the suggestion of new flavors. Not many people yearn for the taste of yarrow, sea buckthorn and tree sap. And yet they flock to Noma, and, if they can't make it there in person, to the *idea* of Noma. The appeal of Redzepi's cooking has to do with a kind of pastoral dream. In a moment when haute cuisine has been summoned to arbitrate our position between technology and nature, Noma comes down firmly on the side of the wild.

It's difficult—and perhaps irresponsible—to critique the food of a restaurant where I have never eaten, and the recipes in a cookbook I can't cook from. (In the interest of service journalism I was going to try to make something from *Noma Recipes*, but without access to mahogany clams, desiccated scallops or reindeer blood, I had to give up.) But I do think it's possible to ask some questions about the meaning of Redzepi's food, especially since the *Journal* gets so deep into the thought processes behind it.

The *Journal* chronicles a year in the life of Noma. It's a constant struggle to make new dishes, hemmed in by two constraints—each has to be both Nordic and seasonal. These constraints impose a series of daunting challenges for the chefs, chief among them the fact that not much really grows in Denmark in winter, and what does hasn't typically been considered fit material for fine dining. In response, Redzepi's team devises a series of inspired workarounds. They find ways to maximize the flavor and longevity of their produce through drying and pickling, discovering such unexpected ingredients as juniper-beech powder and pickled gooseberries. They also begin a whole program of "trash cooking," in which they devise dishes out of fish scales and potato peels.

Redzepi presents cooking at Noma as a process of continual innovation and collaboration. Actually, it's sort of intoxicating to imagine working there—the thought of showing up every day to think about the weather and the seasons, looking for inspiration in the crates of forest mushrooms and live shrimp gathered that morning by bearded fishermen. On Saturday nights, there are jam sessions where the whole staff gets to come up with dishes of their own, like kale ice cream or cucumber dessert (which Redzepi immediately puts on the menu). Not to mention the fact that Redzepi almost bankrupts the restaurant by spending all his profits on remodeling the staff kitchen. All in all, Noma seems like an open, interesting and progressive place to work, one with exactly the kind of internal culture tech companies dream of fostering.

The appeal of Noma as a workplace might actually go some way towards explaining why chefs have become such cultural icons in recent years. In the past decade or two, as Silicon Valley has emerged as the most dynamic sector of the economy, our ideas about aesthetic fulfillment have undergone a subtle transformation. Our models of creativity are no longer struggling loners like painters or novelists. They aren't media figures, like pop stars or movie stars. They're not performers of any kind, for the most part—definitely not dancers, stage actors or classical musicians. More than anything, they're skillful managers and team builders—entrepreneurs like Steve Jobs, architects like Zaha Hadid, chefs like Redzepi. Their mode of work—sociable, engaged, attentive to design, profitable—is immensely appealing, especially to those stuck alone at a desk or computer console.

WHAT NOMA DOESN'T feature much of is actual Scandinavian cooking. Redzepi twice tries to make versions of dishes he remembers from childhood—his Macedonian grandmother's stuffed grape leaves and a

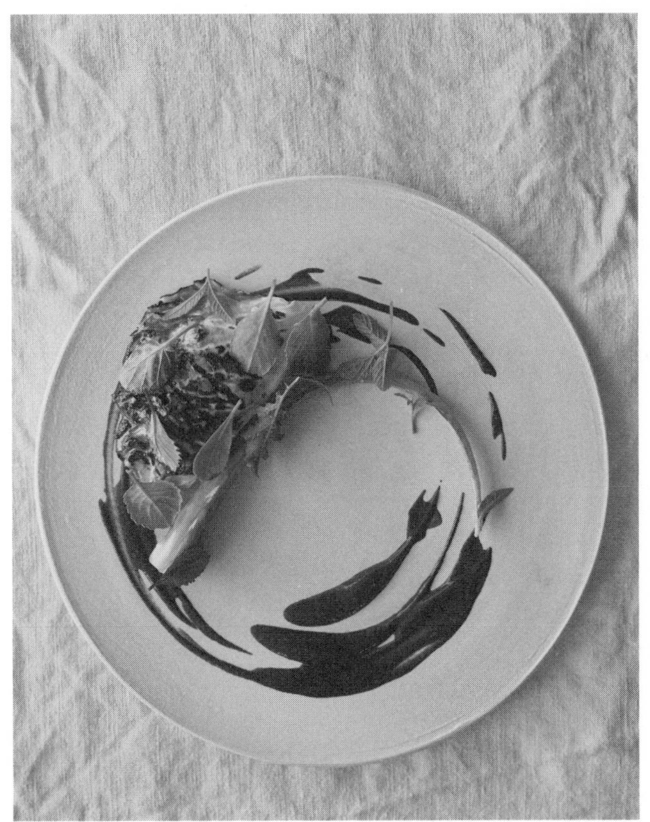

René Redzepi, Water Pike from *A Work in Progress*, 2013

classic Danish dish of game with cream sauce—and both times faces deep skepticism from his staff, who warn him: "Are you sure you want to work on this, chef? It will never be as good as you remember."

But Redzepi avoids direct imitation of classic Nordic fare, just as he approaches the dishes of his youth as obliquely as possible. Those rice-and-meat-stuffed dolmas he remembers from his childhood turn into roasted packets of cabbage leaves filled with pike fillet and verbena sauce. The first time he sees the dish, Redzepi says, "This doesn't look like Macedonia." What he is after isn't an evocation of a memory or a recreation of a particular way of eating. It's not really pastoral either, at its core—at least not in the sense of replicating the foodways of actual peasants or shepherds. What Redzepi is getting at is a vision that has proven to be remarkably seductive in our technological age. His cooking is an attempt to commune with nature in a primal way, to talk directly to the soil and the trees.

One of the most famous dishes at Noma is called Fjord Shrimp with Brown Butter. In it, several live shrimp are served live in glass jars full of ice. The diners pluck them out, dip them in butter and eat them alive. Eating Redzepi's shrimp (or his citrusy live ants) offers more than a flavor or an experience: it offers contact with animality itself. Redzepi admits as much, writing that the butter is "really just for the timid, who want to cover the insect-like eyes and head with a quick nervous dunk"—the real point is the encounter, "predator against prey."

But even more compelling than the animal world in Redzepi's cooking is the idea of the earth. That bite of shrimp contains "an accurate representation of the flavors of the ocean at this exact moment." Similarly, when Noma's chefs prepare wild duck, they serve it covered in beech leaves: a way of imagining its last moments as it falls to its death on the forest floor. Which is what so much of Redzepi's work returns to: the forest floor itself. Hence the attention to soil, grass, mushrooms and wood. In its refusal of culture in the name of nature, Redzepi's cooking reminds me not so much of anything Nordic, but of Teutonic philosophy. In "The Origin of the Work of Art," Martin Heidegger describes a pair of old peasant shoes vibrating with "the silent call of the earth, its quiet gift of the ripening grain and its unexplained self-refusal in the fallow desolation of the wintry field." The earth represents, to Heidegger, a state of being before humans and before language. It's a kind of philosophic no-place at the other end of an experiential abyss. The difficulty of thinking our way into it is the reason it's so hard to answer the question of what it's like to be a bat—or a toad or a rock or a clump of grass. Poets fascinated by the nonhuman realm, like Seamus Heaney and Francis Ponge, try to put this "silent call" into words. In his own peculiar way, Redzepi is attempting to do the same thing, only instead of trying to give it voice, he wants to put it on a plate.

At one point in the *Journal*, Redzepi imagines surprising one of his best customers with an ultimate dish. But it isn't so much a dish as an experience:

> that wonderful sensation of walking through the woods on fields of wet moss. I want to take these pieces of moss, cleaned, dried and simmered in juniper broth, and sprinkle them with dried berries, forest plant, juniper oil, cep oil, thyme oil—anything delicious from the woods. I imagine Ali, looking down into the bowl at what looks like wet moss, then at his spoon, back to the bowl, and glancing up with a scared look, asking "what should I do?"

So this is Redzepi's wish: to put a piece of ground in front of a diner and have him figure it out. And once you got over your dismay at being served moss on a plate, maybe you would. His cooking is an attempt to go beyond the world of language and culture and into the world of pure things. And like any real artist, Redzepi articulates desires we didn't even know we had—not for nutritive powders or engineered foams, but for contact with another way of being. To taste the essence of rocks and trees, to creep through the forest like a snail, to sleep in the earth like onions, with our feet in the air.

Ian Martin, from *Kranshoek Township* series, 2005

NORMAN RUSH

by Charles Finch

THE NOVEL IS a medium of endless permutations, but in the end there are three broad ways that it can be great. The first and lowest is on the level of sheer craft. *Pride and Prejudice*, *The Fault in Our Stars*, *Madame Bovary*, *Jurassic Park*—simply as machines, all of these are close to flawless. They pull the reader through their structure remorselessly; their characters serve their stories; they're filled at once with surprise and inevitability.

On a different plane is the third, highest way in which a novel can be great: it can teach us something about existing as a human being in the world. I don't think there's much point in elaborating on this idea, because while we mostly start out with the same names—Proust, Mann, Tolstoy—each serious reader refines this definition of genius individually, in a sense even privately. *Madame Bovary* and *Pride and Prejudice* have it, for me.

Then there's the second way.

Last year the great American novelist Norman Rush published a new book, *Subtle Bodies*, his fourth. Unlike the first three—*Whites*, *Mating* and *Mortals*—it is not set in Botswana, where Rush and his wife Elsa were Peace Corps co-directors from 1978 to 1983, and perhaps that missing edge of novelty is one reason why there's been a tone of civil disappointment in the critical response. Nevertheless all four books are of a piece, sharing a pair of central concerns: geopolitics, specifically with regard to issues of structural injustice, and the nature of a long and extremely intimate marriage.

On those first and third levels of the art of the novel, Rush is only an equivocal and intermittent master. Passages of his books, particularly *Mortals*, are beautifully plotted, but none of them could be called compulsive from first to last solely by virtue of their story. As for his vision of the world, fascinating though it is, it has limitations of perspective that the best and most dispassionate novelists (even seemingly inward ones, such as Kafka) have been able to transcend. To be specific: few of the humans who populate Rush's books ever seem quite as real as the husband and wife who recur again and again as central characters, bandits traveling under different names each time, and who form the twinned consciousness of his art.

But the second, intermediate level of novelistic greatness has to do with neither technical nor visionary genius. Instead it occurs within the sentence-to-sentence life of a book, in the enormous linked series of thoughts and gestures that make up any novel. Rush is an example of an artist—Iris Murdoch and Robert Musil are others—whose excellence is clearest not in the gestalt of those thoughts and gestures, but in the midst of them, as the pages pass. When critics speak of his genius (James Wood has called him "the most neglected major writer in America") they are testifying to the power and unexpectedness of the hundreds of essayistic accompaniments that proliferate across his work.

These kinds of observations run into every corner of Rush's books, almost too profuse to record as they pass:

- And as for French, he couldn't wait for it to become a dead language, since no nation, a nation of peacocks, had ever deserved it more. It was coming, they knew it and were hysterical about it, but adieu, adieu.

- I have a certain inordinate feeling toward revolutionaries who wear glasses, because there is the sense of how easily they could be unhorsed in the slightest physical confrontation with the enemy just by someone flicking their glasses to the ground and stepping on them. So you assume such people have unusual amounts of courage.

- What did the Batswana find funny? What? He was at a loss. He did know they thought it was funny to say of a man married to harridan that he ate his overcoat. ... It was conceivable that a whole people would find nothing funny in the jokes of their what, their oppressors, their colonial masters, their laughing master ... It was possible there was nothing universal about humor.

- He pitied serious writers. The best that 99 percent of them could hope for was a glancing appearance in a survey course at lengthening intervals. Even Milton was dropping to survey status more and more, even at the graduate level. It was true. And the next step down would be the collateral reading in a survey course, the books only the strivers got around to ... and then it would be down to a footnote in a title in the collateral list. And then what, some academic trivia game. And then nothing.

Realizing the primacy of simple *opinion* in Rush's work, of analysis and declaration, makes the nature of his particular gifts easier to articulate. By such a reading, he seems not the heir to whatever thwarted tradition of the novel one might hazard (Dostoevsky, Conrad, Greene); nor does he seem to have very much to do with Roth or Updike, despite sharing with them a generational identity and plenty of bedroom voyeurism. Instead, he would descend from an older, alternate ancestry, one belonging to the aphorists and essayists of world literature:

Pascal, Leopardi, Montaigne. None of those writers are novelists, of course, and part of what makes Rush unusual is that he's successfully embedded their legacy of interpolation, their faith in lateral thought, into classic realist fiction—a risk that many novelists have rightly been reluctant to take. The reward is that in Rush's novels there is the constant possibility that the next sentence is about to tell us something new.

ONE OF THE many unusual things about Rush's career is that he didn't publish his first book until he was 53. The book was *Whites* (1986), a collection of stories about quasi-colonials in Botswana, whites without the full reach of colonial power, mostly attached to aid and governmental organizations. Its first story, "Bruns," was published in the *New Yorker*, and immediately won Rush a powerful agent, Andrew Wylie, and subsequently a contract at Knopf. Five years later he published *Mating* (1991), the story of a love affair in a planned feminist community in Botswana, and twelve years after that another novel about the country, *Mortals* (2003), this time involving a CIA agent and a local insurrection. Rush has a reputation for working slowly, but in fact it's these three books, all set in the same place, all concerning the same social milieu, and all published in the brief range between his fifty-third and seventieth years, that have given him his titanic reputation.

Why did his career take so long to begin in earnest?

Rush has described his early work on several occasions. "At Swarthmore I published some gnomic poems based on little-known events in the tragic history of the democratic Left," he's said, and later, "I wrote agonizingly experimental stories that simply baffled editors." In the 1970s he found some success with short fiction but not with a novel, *Equals*, about an experimental college. For much of his adult life he was a rare-book dealer and a political activist. (Rush's roots are in Oakland, and there's a Lebowski-ish note to his pre-Africa life, noble but comic: "I was for years on the boards of the Central Committee for Conscientious Objectors and the War Registers League, and was active in CORE, the Congress of Racial Equality.")

It was going to Botswana that changed Rush, aerating his fiction by liberating him from what seems as if it was a passionate but cramped worldview. Tellingly, he burned all of his early writing in 1978, the year he left. That he went at all was an accident. As he tells the story:

> Botswana was a fluke ... We knew Sam Brown, an antiwar activist, whom Carter had appointed head of ACTION, the umbrella agency for the Peace Corps. But I didn't know of his appointment at this dinner party where Sam and Elsa and I got into a political argument ... We must have impressed Sam as being qualified, though I don't know how ... he set up a day of interviews for us in D.C. We figured we had no chance but that the interviews would be fun. They wanted people with Ph.D.'s in economics, or development studies, or at least some work overseas ... We had nothing to lose, and so we killed all day ... The question then became where we should go. Because we each had had six years of school French, they planned to send us to Francophone Africa. We proposed Benin, but were mistakenly delivered to a different B desk, the Botswana one. The Botswana desk officer liked us, and unbeknownst to us, put in a request as soon as we left.

This immense aleatory change in Rush's life—a dinner party, a mix-up of desks—is exactly the kind of incident that fills his fiction about the country where he and Elsa moved, and where at once life seems looser and less reliable, more chancy, but therefore also fuller. (The opening line of *Mating* is famous: "In Africa, you want more, I think.") The move gave him a subject for study other than his own anguished opinions, and a language—fans of Rush will carry certain words (*rra*, *mealie*, *Batswana*, *gosiame*) to the ends of their days—to at once sharpen and loosen his prose. "It was nerve-racking, exciting and it was nonstop," he told the *Paris Review*. "I returned to America with cartons of material."

And yet his opinions are still what matter about Rush's fiction; the external shock of moving to Botswana, and of the arduous work he did there, merely freed them from their moorings in sixties radicalism. His moral and anthropological sense of the world finally had a vehicle to bear it into written thought.

The works that show it best are *Mating* and *Mortals*. Now that Rush is 80, the shape of his career seems to make that plain, with *Whites*, for all its brilliance, a mere warning shot signaling the two huge novels he would write, and *Subtle Bodies* a problematic contrail. In assessing him I think it's worth considering *Mating* and *Mortals* most closely—the first for its perfections, the second, after a thirteen-year silence from the author, both for the reemergence of those perfections and for a theretofore unseen set of associated limitations.

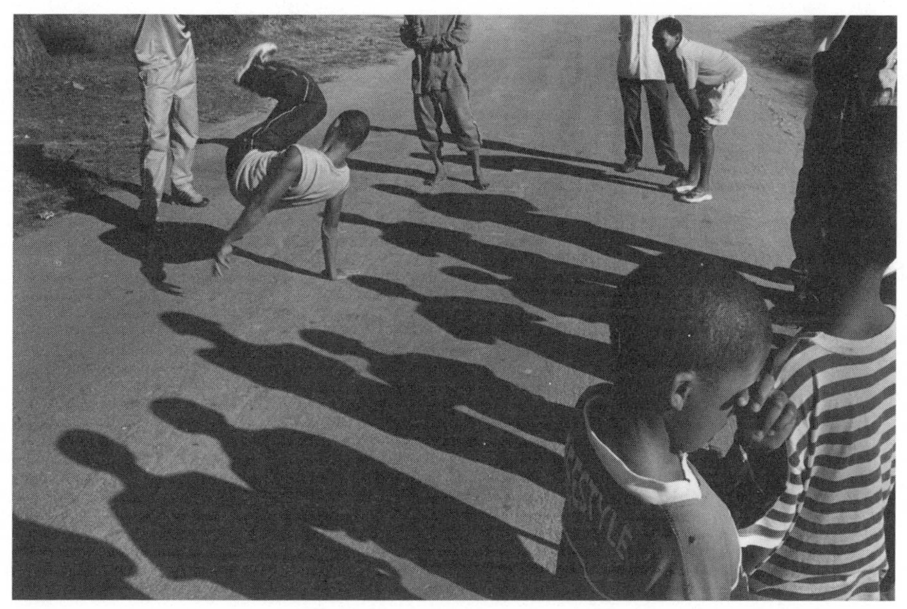

Ian Martin, from *Kranshoek Township* series, 2005

THE NARRATOR OF *Mating* (1991) is one of the great achievements of twentieth-century fiction. In the course of a very long novel she never names herself. An anthropologist from Stanford doing fieldwork in Gaborone, her language is erudite, dry and full of proud self-taught texture. (A partial list of the Latin phrases she uses, some dozens of times each: *id est*, *cumo grano salis*, *ultra vires*, *suave mare magno*, *inter pocula*. Or of her stranger words: *anorectic*, *lustration*, *megrim*, *undsoweiter*, *ruck*, *cryptomnesia*, *urticarial*, *vitromania*.) She yearns for love too, however, and finds the potential object of it quickly—Nelson DeNoon, an older anthropologist, famous for his past academic work but now engaged in a secretive communal project in the Botswana countryside.

The narrator sets out alone to find DeNoon in the first third of the book, and her solitary voyage across the desert, filled with moments of danger and hallucination, is a transcendent passage of fiction. "Anyone who thinks crossing the Kalahari by yourself is boring is deluded," she says. "It's like being self-employed in a marginal enterprise: there's always something you should be doing if your little business is going to survive." Later she loses one of her donkeys and begins to face real trouble. "I dawdled breaking camp because I wanted to give any lions there were a head start at getting torpid. Lions are torpid during the day, was a key part of my lore package."

The brilliance of this character—in *Mortals* we learn that her name is likely Karen—is that she's literate without being literary. (It must have taken Rush restraint to write lines like this: "Whoever said he had measured out his life in coffee spoons was talking about me that day.") Instead her voice is that of a social scientist's, giving cover both to Rush's literary aims and to the character's own weaknesses and fears, which emerge with exquisite and unliterary unhurriedness. There's the anxiety of her language, for example. In addition to all that Latin, the words "naturally" and "obviously" and "of course" recur, signaling a haste for self-identification as intelligent which is rooted in class memories, as this aside, heart-wrenching from a person we know to be so practical and illusionless, conveys:

> Status in my high school came from how infrequently you wore the same clothes, and especially how infrequently you wore the same sweaters. In my humble opinion life shouldn't be more painful than it has to be. I remember all the desperate improvisations and camouflages it took to disguise the dreadful brevity of the little cycle of clothes I had to wear. This still has the capacity to freeze my heart.

That need for self-proof is also what sends her after DeNoon, and when she finds him the book finds communion with its author's greater political energies, to spectacular effect; DeNoon's planned community, Tsau, is a stroke of brilliance, because it allows Rush to lay out, organically, his hundreds of small theories of human society, human love.

Some of these are charming—for instance, every house in Tsau has a lantern outside, which when lit indicates that its inhabitants would like to receive guests that evening. More often, however, the theories are driven by a will toward redress on behalf of women, who run the village and are the only citizens permitted to inherit property. (DeNoon loathes with particular fury the "the idea that women are just pontoons for the various male enterprises coming down the pike.") In a less subtle writer the representation of such a mission might become hectoringly meliorist, but Rush has too sophisticated a sense of human balance for that; as *Mating* moves forward many of the women of Tsau, and indeed the narrator, gradually begin to cede their institutional power to men—on behalf of the impulses of love, that is, of mating. This is the doubleness we ought to seek in a writer: when Rush is most persuasive about Tsau's vision of the possibilities of civil progress, he is also relinquishing some of his claims for it. Ideas in fiction are more potent when they don't come armored against their own contradictions.

The ideas in Rush's second novel, *Mortals*, are as subtle and rich as those in *Mating*. But there is something slightly diminished in its ultimate effect by comparison; unlike the earlier book, *Mortals* is written in the third-person, and it is perhaps in this transition that a glimmer of trouble appears. Every mode of narration has its virtues and defects, of course, and there may be readers who find the first-person of *Mating* claustrophobic. What it offered Rush, however, was concealment—a means of expression for his own fascinating, intercalating, uniquely essayistic voice, which nevertheless, because a reader could ascribe all of its decrees to the narrator, existed naturalistically within the novel.

The free indirect voice offers Rush some shell for this style, but not enough. In *Mortals* it becomes a minor problem; in *Subtle Bodies*, very nearly a fatal one. That's the blemish on Rush's career, perhaps, an inability to recede behind his characters. The constant interruption of opinion into his work means that he never quite vanishes into the third person and therefore never achieves the fluid multivocalism that gives each character equal weight, what Bakhtin praised as polyphony. Rush's natural pendant, another white-bearded novelist of lower Africa, J. M. Coetzee, is by contrast exquisitely skillful at self-concealment, at the neutral clarities of third-person fiction. By either method there is some price to pay. In Coetzee's case it's a chilliness; in Rush's, a diminution of realism. Rush's loss may be the greater.

But before returning to this problem it's worth describing what *Mortals* does seriously and uniquely and well, which is to assess American morality within the context of Africa's post-colonial history. The book's hero is Ray Finch, a professor in Gaborone who also works undercover for the CIA. He's married to a woman with whom he's ardently in love, Iris, and though she loves her husband too, she's not quite happy in Botswana, and comes under the sway of an African American doctor named Davis Morel. Morel has come to Botswana, armed with literature, to preach to the locals against Christianity.

The first half of *Mortals* is about Ray's dawning suspicion that Iris may be sleeping with Morel; the second half is about a bloody, terrifying political insurrection into which Ray and Morel are drawn, together, north of Gaborone. This summary sounds dry, but the insurrection itself is thrilling—the scenes are full of basic, practical problems that Ray and Morel are forced to solve together, but which are constantly shadowed by their personal and spiritual conflict with each other. In their exhausting bloody action, these passages become a kind of silent rebuke to the American cultural ideal of emancipation through action and violence (which Rush himself has associated, without much enthusiasm, with "the vitalist tradition" of writers like Crane, Mailer and Robert Stone). War is a physical, not a soteriological, experience. The consequences of it live on in individual bodies, first and foremost, and then in long-term civic fracture, which outlives by centuries any fleeting sense of personal liberation.

Rush lets the significance of that message in an African setting—a setting whose historical proof it is—dawn on the reader slowly, and therefore devastatingly. *Mortals* is the fullest expression of his ideas about Africa, which are deeply structuralist, absorbed with the patterns by which community and nationality subdue individual agency. "A true holocaust in the world is the thing we call development," Rush writes, by which he means "the superimposition of market economies on traditional and unprepared third world cultures by force and fraud circa 1880 to the present." Are the whites of his books (he told the *New York Times* that it was essential for him to write about Africa by way of "Americans and Americanity") replicating this holocaust, or repairing it? *Mating* offers an anthropological assessment, and *Mortals* offers a political one, both deeply persuasive.

What remains intact in the later book is Rush's voice, whose sheer contour of thought is again an overwhelming success. And yet it contains forewarnings, too, of what makes *Subtle Bodies* so much less successful than the work that preceded it.

All three of Rush's novels are about the relationship between a woman in her thirties and a man at least a decade older, and in all three the pair are overwhelmingly, consumingly in love. (It's part of their lore package that Nor-

Ian Martin, from *Kranshoek Township* series, 2005

man and Elsa Rush are, too.) In *Mortals*, this has the effect of making the book seem slightly gaga. Iris's physical beauty is constantly reiterated, and takes on an almost Ayn Randian conflation of attractiveness with quality of character—Ray thinks at one point of "someone at her level of physical beauty dealing with people so much more nicely than she should be," and later is conscious that he is "talking to the most beautiful white woman in southern Africa, outside of the movies." And on and on.

The cost of this deep focus on a single couple is that, like Rush's interjecting voice, it works toward the exclusion of other characters, so that for instance Davis Morel and the heroic Kerekang of *Mortals* never quite seem like more than externalities of the marriage at the heart of the book. Was it the experience of being alone with his wife in Botswana for five years that pushed Rush so far into his wife's mind and spirit, giving a faint dreamishness to everyone except the Adam and Eve he models in his last two books? Perhaps. As Ray puts it, more poignantly, "It was the fear of being left alone in Africa, where nobody loved you."

Whatever the reason, by the time we get to the central couple in *Subtle Bodies*, Ned and Nina, they have narrowed so far into each other, and into their love, that the reader is left with nothing outside of them. It feels like a book in which the author has lost the sense of distance that ought to exist between himself, his characters and his readers. Its universe of secondary characters—they're gathered in upstate New York for the funeral of an old college friend of Ned's—collapses into itself, until Rush's observations, which were integrated so seamlessly into Karen's voice in *Mating*, and which were mostly attributable to Ray Finch in *Mortals*, come to seem almost wholly freestanding, nothing to do with the texture of the novel's marriage-story. It's true that those observations remain sharp—a shrewd recapitulation of what many people felt during America in the 2000s. (Ned has a "revenge fantasy" that every time George W. Bush tells a joke for the remainder of his life, "stinking bloody arms and legs and heads and feet would fall on him.") But the familiarity of those politics makes even the most intelligent take on them feel less fresh than anything in *Mortals* or *Mating*. Those gnomic poems, that novel about an experimental college and this book—it may be that Rush did need Botswana to write effectively, after all.

AS HE WAS composing *Subtle Bodies*, Rush told an interviewer:

> I must love big novels, because that's what I've written ... In the book I'm working on now, though, I'm trying to keep everything shorter: shorter scenes, fewer plots, general brevity. But a shorter novel goes against some of my deepest instincts. Dostoevsky died still intending to write another volume of *The Brothers Karamazov*. It's like a knife in my heart that he didn't.

This quote, with its explicit anxiety about the decision to shape *Subtle Bodies* differently from its predecessors, brings the book's flaws into clearer sight: Rush has so much to tell us (that side word about Dostoevsky is quintessential) that even when he aims for brevity, all of his opinions, his puns and palindromes, his digressions, force their way into the text anyhow, whether they belong or not. (*Whites* is an exception because many of its stories are closely focused on single incidents.) In *Subtle Bodies*, his first short novel, that surfeit becomes a defect rather than a virtue for the first time.

But an author's failures can be instructive. Cervantes believed his best work was *The Labors of Persiles and Sigismunda*, a romance whose characters are flat enough that they could have won Don Quixote's affection. By overcrowding a short novel with his own thoughts, Rush shows, inadvertently, how essential the form of the long novel was to his development.

One of the glories of the long novel is that as it progresses there's less and less space for fakery. In a short novel, verve and cleverness can stand in for the actually meaningful—think of Paul Auster, tossing out free-ranging signifiers without taking responsibility for what they might signify, or César Aira and his charming but maddening *fuga hacia adelante*. Obviously there are numerous short novels without an ounce of fraud in them, but it's also true that the further a novel extends, the more obvious any vagueness of intention or thought becomes. Roberto Bolaño and David Foster Wallace are correctly revered because of their ability to sustain for far longer than most writers a simultaneous pitch of enigma and lucidity.

Stylistically, then, the long novel is ideal for an author whose most essential mission, regardless of subject matter, is honesty—is disclosure. "I love demystification inordinately," the narrator of *Mating* says, and later adds:

MFA
VS
NYC

> I hate the mysterious because it's the perfect medium for liars, the place they go to multiply and preen and lie to each other. Liars are the enemy. They transcend class, sex, and nation. They make everything impossible.

It might seem that Rush's preference for small generalizations, his essayistic style, would muddle the intelligibility of his novels, but in fact precisely the opposite is true. There are few more mystified places than Africa, and few more mystified subjects than love; *Mating* and *Mortals* gain their marvelous strength from their fusion and subsequent demystification of the two, which is exacted in part by their gradual but continuous rejection, over many hundreds of pages, of cant. There are many novels that offer a more encompassing vision of life than Rush's, but few so insistent upon clarity, upon transmission.

This insistence on clarity is a trait that belongs both to Rush and to his most successful characters. There's a moment in *Mortals* when Ray fears for his marriage and is tempted to ignore his suspicion but then thinks, in a spasm of moral bravery that seems to the reader (who knows Ray's incredible passion for his wife) as substantial as any of the book's acts of physical bravery, "Thought looks into the face of hell and is not afraid." That single line defines Norman Rush's ethic, I think—and given the granular energy of his novels, their thousand discrete interrogations of the world, it describes too both the consciousness and the courage he demands of his readers.

Krista van der Niet, *Theedoek 1*, 2013

CHARLIE TROTTER

by Gordon Arlen

CHARLIE TROTTER PIONEERED that style of fine dining now beloved by foodies from Brooklyn to the Bay Area: an intense progression of small, seasonal, multicourse dishes with perfectly balanced but explosive flavors matched against expert wine pairings; the use of offal and other "nose-to-tail" butchering methods; integration of French technique with Asian spicing; the use of savory ingredients in dessert courses; the replacement of cream and butter with lighter vegetable-based purées and emulsions. Named best in the world by *Wine Spectator* magazine in 1998, just as the Bulls were completing their championship run, Trotter's eponymous restaurant brought him worldwide fame and a Jordan-like status in Chicago, and by the time of his premature death in 2013, aged 54, he had multiple cookbooks and a television show to his name.

Yet within the world of celebrity chefs Trotter was considered an enigma. A political science major from the University of Wisconsin with no formal culinary training, he was known to quote Dostoevsky and Kierkegaard and screen avant-garde movies for staff before dinner service. He named his son after Bob Dylan and spent time in the acid-laced Madison of the early 1980s, but once complained about the demise of American formality: "People no longer dress up on airplanes."

That last remark was made to me personally, and the following reflections are informed by my experience getting to know Trotter, both inside and outside his restaurant, over the last three years of his life. On my first visit to the brownstone at 814 W. Armitage, I found Trotter's food to be light, ethereal and floral; it kept me stimulated and alert, with the build up and release of creative tension characteristic of great symphonies. It hit me in the head before the stomach—the world's most expensive brain food, I joked.

IT HAS BECOME commonplace to think of chefs as more than kitchen technicians; they are bubbly personalities, from the girl next door (Rachael Ray) to the jocular Italian with orange Crocs (Mario Batali); mad scientists armed with liquid nitrogen and other toys (Grant Achatz, Heston Blumenthal); travel writers and ambassadors of globalization (Anthony Bourdain); impressionist artists (Pierre Gagnaire); farm-to-table naturalists (Alice Waters); postmodern nationalists (René Redzepi). None of these roles entirely captures Trotter.

He certainly had a reputation as a Gordon Ramsay-style kitchen disciplinarian, lampooned in his fiery "mad chef" cameo in the 1997 movie *My Best Friend's Wedding*. I don't believe he was tyrannical in the sense of loving power for its own sake. But he ruled his restaurant by imposing exacting standards. Hospitality was predicated upon submission. Customers were not always right. Stories abound of Trotter emerging from the kitchen to confront customers who had failed to finish everything on their plate. With every morsel contributing to the form, leaving something uneaten was the ultimate philistinism.

What became clear to me over time was that if there was discipline it was for a purpose. The entire restaurant had a hushed feel, with no artwork or music: focus had to stay on the food. Staff were impeccably dressed and sometimes even forced to wear special shoe guards to avoid tracking dirt; wine was served on glistening Riedel crystal stemware. Trotter's mission was to construct a temple of sensory elevation, and a temple must be kept pure.

LIKE ANY SAGE, Trotter cultivated disciples, in his own memorable way. After several visits, managers must have alerted him that a young academic was frequenting his restaurant; I was stunned when the chef emerged from the kitchen and sat down at my table. With envious diners looking on, he sized me up: "I've been told you're a Ph.D. student."

"Yes, I study political theory."

"Then what are you doing here? Shouldn't you be off somewhere reading Nietzsche with a glass of cheap red wine?"

"Well, the truth is, chef, I find your food intellectually satisfying."

He chuckled, as if to say *you don't have to tell me that*. After some small talk Trotter stood up: "I want to get you something. But it's at my house a few blocks away. Hold tight." Ten minutes later he reemerged clutching the Charles Bukowski volume *Notes of a Dirty Old Man*. He plopped it next to my plate, the tattered book strikingly juxtaposed against the pristine white tablecloth. "You've heard of Bukowski, right?"

"Yeah, though I'm not too familiar with his writing."

"Well I've got an idea: I want you to come work a dinner service in my kitchen. It's an experience I usually auction off for charity, but you can do it for free."

Nervous excitement ensued. "Really? But I don't have any experience, I barely do any serious home cooking."

"Don't worry," he assured me. "You're smart, that's what matters. I do have one request though. I want you to take a look at the Bukowski. Here, I'll loan you my copy."

I was flabbergasted: How could Bukowski's sordid tales of life in underworld Los Angeles prepare me for dinner service in one of the world's most renowned kitchens? A few weeks later, I reported for duty at 3 p.m., half expecting a literature exam. But Trotter was all business on this busy Saturday. "Clean yourself up," he barked, as I struggled to properly tie my apron. Assigned to a sous chef, I was placed on the hot line, where I almost started a stove fire. Instead of demotion I was handed even more responsibility. Somehow I survived, staying until 3 a.m. to help with the scrub-down. It was twelve hours of extreme physical exertion—blaring heat, no chance to sit. But it was exhilarating to witness the precise choreography of the young, sophisticated staff. One especially graceful wine steward, with a background in ballet and Chinese opera, had been hired right out of academia. "You can work here too if you want, Gordon," she insisted. "Charlie looks for qualities they don't teach in culinary school." I began to wonder if the whole evening had been a job interview.

In truth, one night in the apron was more than enough. But I returned a number of times as a diner, with Trotter often directing the conversation to philosophy or literature before I ever had the chance to ask him about the food being served. These visits became a kind of pilgrimage; I realized that the man was just as interesting as his cuisine.

CHARLIE TROTTER WAS raised in the affluent Chicago suburb of Winnetka, attending the prestigious New Trier High School. At age 27 he opened the restaurant with capital from his father Bob; in a historically blue-collar profession in which even talented chefs must work for others, Charlie thus had the decided advantage of working for himself. Bob also instilled in his son an appreciation for jazz, and Charlie came to see cooking as an improvisational art, a sequence of "Kitchen Sessions," as he called his PBS television show. Like the jazz greats Miles Davis and Charlie Parker (for whom he was named), Trotter was intent on proving that an improvisational aesthetic can still be structured and responsive to form. He therefore had no signature dishes like Thomas Keller's "oysters and pearls." The investment banker Ray Harris,

Trotter's most loyal devotee, famously dined at the restaurant over 400 times and was never served the same dish twice.

This demanding aesthetic was difficult to translate into commercial empire. A 1994 venture at the MGM Grand in Las Vegas shuttered in part because Trotter resisted pressures to dumb down his cuisine—"a little more steak please." Indeed, in a carnivore nation, vegetables became the stars of Trotter's craft. Alan Richman, the GQ food critic, once credited Trotter for proving vegetables can taste good and be beautiful. It has become a cliché for chefs to tout their commitment to "artisanal," "organic" and "farm-to-table" cooking; but there was nothing clichéd about Trotter's eight-course vegetable tasting menus, which I often preferred to his meat-based menus. Serving them on glistening china in breathtaking visual preparations, Trotter had a knack for making vegetables luxurious and decadent without jeopardizing their essential earthiness. I enjoyed dishes such as "miso tortellini with red cabbage, turnip confit and ponzu" and "salad of Bibb lettuce with candied peanut, sesame and heart of palm ice cream." A raw vegan menu was even available every night on request. These practices were borne less of a political commitment to "sustainability" or a nutritional commitment to healthy living than of an aesthetic commitment to vegetables as a frontier in the quest for purity. That quest meant Trotter had no tolerance for adjusting his cuisine to the constraints of localism. Tasmanian ocean trout was procured at great expense, he explained, simply because the waters off Tasmania are the cleanest in the world.

Despite these innovations, Trotter struggled to confront the rise of "molecular gastronomy"—the style of cooking mastered by Grant Achatz, a former Trotter line cook whose acclaimed restaurant Alinea (located only a few blocks away) became Trotter's main rival. Molecular gastronomy is a postmodern, deconstructive art, with engineering techniques being used to manipulate ingredients into untold textures and temperatures. Beauty is found in the realization that chocolates and spring peas maintain the same chemistry regardless of how they have been fabricated. Once molecular patterns have been discovered they can be perfected, reproduced and even trademarked (in the case of packaged food companies whose test kitchens employ many techniques perfected at Alinea). Trotter, by contrast, was more of a modernist: while intensely creative, he respected the basic forms of *nouvelle* French cuisine which had governed fine dining for much of the late twentieth century. He venerated Fernand Point, author of the modernist bible *Ma Gastronomie*. Thus Trotter's resistance to molecular gastronomy as "nonsense on stilts" (he banned liquid nitrogen in his kitchen) was the defining aesthetic judgment of his career. He stubbornly maintained the integrity of his form despite the risk of being left behind.

Krista van der Niet, *Theedoek 3*, 2013

Trotter did have a libertarian side that relished marketplace validation. Regarding the ethics of charging people $300 for food and wine, he insisted his restaurant was one of the few luxury experiences accessible to ordinary people, if only once in their lifetime ("no more expensive than a good plumber"). But Trotter was also charitable. Through his "Excellence Program" he would invite Chicago public school students to the restaurant free of charge to enjoy the same eight-course meal offered to customers. He also regularly fed homeless people. Trotter likely could have satisfied the homeless with warm soup; his insistence on serving them a Michelin-star meal underscores that his philanthropy had sensory objectives.

IN A WORLD where Yelp and Twitter offer a never-ending array of subjective valuations, and in a field that would seem to be the home of subjective valuation—who can say whether strawberry ice cream is better than raspberry?—Trotter doggedly upheld the idea of objective value. He was a master craftsman who searched for *knowledge*.

Outside the kitchen I experienced firsthand what Plato would have called Trotter's philosophical *eros*, his passion for objective truth. A year or so before his death, Trotter announced his intention to close the restaurant and pursue a graduate degree in philosophy. He asked me for advice. On a cold February morning I met him at the parking lot of the University of Chicago campus for what became a five-hour tour. "Can people be arrested for bad architecture?" he quipped as we passed the brutalist Regenstein Library. Yet as the campus's beautiful gothic core emerged, Trotter quieted down, as if awed by the immense splendor of a temple outranking his own. Meeting with several faculty I was struck by the shy, almost nervous demeanor of a man who could be so intimidating. "I have no agenda" Trotter insisted, "I just want to pursue the life of the mind." But Trotter had a learning disability, a serious case of dyslexia. He never masked this dyslexia, often crediting it for helping him see food in a different light. But graduate school would be a different challenge. Professor Nathan Tarcov reminded Trotter that Allan Bloom, the great Plato translator, was also dyslexic; as Malcolm Gladwell has recently suggested, it can force one to read closely. But I think Trotter knew that he was not Allan Bloom, nor Nathan Tarcov his host, nor even Gordon Arlen, his graduate student tour guide. There was no easy path from the temple at 814 W. Armitage to the temple on the quad.

systems/process by willy chyr

As we returned to the parking lot, Trotter insisted on dropping me off in his Jaguar; with dinner service only a few hours away, his confidence began to reemerge. That evening, at 2 a.m., I received a voice message: "Hey Gordon, it's Charlie. Look, what you did for me today was amazing. Why don't you come over to my house this Sunday? We can play pool, maybe have a bite to eat."

Sure enough, that Sunday I trudged over to Trotter's Lincoln Park townhouse for an intimate gathering. Trotter took me around the entire house, even to his bedroom. He lay back against his gregarious wife Rochelle, a pastor's daughter from Chicago's West Side and herself an accomplished culinarian and television personality, as she told a story about their experience cooking for Arab royalty. Dinner was delivered from Trotter's To Go, the chef's more homestyle take-out emporium. We sat at the kitchen counter, with Trotter standing up in perfect posture, as I'm told he often ate. I studied his hands in motion as he carefully prepared for me a simple plate of duck breast, salmon and veggies. Afterwards he presented a goodie bag of amazing foodstuffs, including artisanal canned tuna from Spain ("open it in a few months and it will rock your world").

Before leaving I reciprocated by presenting Trotter with a copy of an anthology called *The History of Political Philosophy*. "It's difficult reading," I warned, "but it might help you determine which thinkers to explore more fully." He clutched the book firmly to his body, his face betraying genuine emotion, and placed it on his bedroom shelf. "This means the world to me," he said, "though it will take a year for me to read." The gift seemed to symbolize a rite of passage to the contemplative life he so desired.

FOURTEEN MONTHS AFTER our last contact, Trotter was found unresponsive in the same bedroom that housed the anthology. In the months since, Rochelle Trotter has announced plans for an "institute of learning"—the Charlie Trotter Center for Excellence—to provide lectures and seminars for at-risk youth interested in the culinary field. A centerpiece of this project will be a "floating library," perhaps tied to an institution like the James Beard Foundation, to house Trotter's voluminous collection of 1,400 cookbooks and 600 fiction and nonfiction titles. The legacy of a chef who created so much sensual pleasure in his time will be preserved, at least in part, through his dusty collection of Bukowski novels and Plato dialogues.

There is no doubt that Trotter became frustrated with the increasingly faddish nature of a culinary landscape held hostage to the ever-changing preferences of foodies. "Everybody's always looking for the next big thing," he once told me. But I wonder whether this anxiety opened out into a reflection on the ephemeral nature of the craft itself. Food leaves no indelible mark; nobody will ever again share in the experience of his cuisine as it was served. Perhaps Trotter realized that. Perhaps his longing for the contemplative life was, in the end, a longing for something more durable.

CARL VAN VECHTEN'S PHOTOGRAPHY

by J. C. Gabel

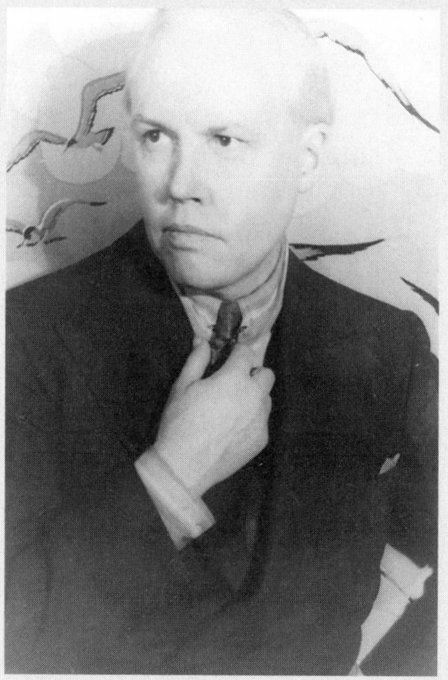

Carl Van Vechten, *Self-portrait*, 1934

LATE IN 2013, as it does every year, the Oxford English Dictionary announced its Word of the Year. It was "selfie," which the OED defined this way on its website: "*noun, informal* (also selfy; plural selfies) a photograph that one has taken of oneself, typically one taken with a smartphone or webcam and uploaded to a social media website."

Carl Van Vechten passed away fifty years ago at the age of 84. If he were alive today, I think he would have enjoyed the idea of the selfie. In the last thirty years of his life, as the modern handheld camera came on the scene, Van Vechten, having observed the easy-to-produce images made possible with a Leica, reinvented himself as a portrait photographer, capturing cultural personalities as well as himself. He was keen on taking self-portraits, the selfies of his time.

In the first half of the twentieth century, Van Vechten connected myriad cultural dots, as Edward White points out in his thoroughly researched new biography, *The Tastemaker: Carl Van Vechten and the Birth of Modern America*. Like many legendary New Yorkers, Van Vechten hailed from elsewhere—in his case, Cedar Rapids, Iowa, a progressive Midwestern farm town around the time he was born in 1880. His parents were freethinkers of Dutch descent who settled on the prairie after the Civil War, but their roots in America go back to the early days of the colonies. "His one burning desire," White writes of Van Vechten, "was to ditch the life of a bourgeois Midwesterner for the glamour and grime of the big cities."

He did just that: first escaping to Chicago, where he discovered the burgeoning classical music and opera scenes, as well as the African-American communities of the South Side, which thrived from the early Aughts to the 1940s, owing to migration (mostly from the Jim Crow South) and industrialization. In 1906, a few years after graduating from the University of Chicago, Van Vechten left the city for New York, where he would live until his death. There he was, at various stages: a journalist, provocateur novelist, nightlife denizen, music and theater critic, confidant to Gertrude Stein, patron of the Harlem Renaissance, literary dandy, urban impresario, portrait photographer, archivist of modernism and altogether man-about-town.

"Through his life of indulgence and excess, and in promoting his bespoke pantheon of celebrities," writes White in his prologue, "Van Vechten was one of the leading figures of a brash, iconoclastic generation of writers, artists, and thinkers that helped Americans see that art and beauty existed amid the hum and buzz of their own cities and not just in the galleries and theaters of ancient European capitals. His life and legacy have been overlooked simply because of the extraordinary range of his interests."

Blanche and Alfred Knopf, 1932

VAN VECHTEN'S EMBRACE and zealous promotion of the African-American community—especially in Prohibition-era Harlem—is what he is most remembered for today, a point White expounds on throughout the second half of this biography, pulling from Van Vechten's daybook entries, as well as scores of letters he left behind. Not only did Van Vechten champion black artists to the white upper crust of Manhattan, he singlehandedly helped the writers Nella Larsen, Langston Hughes and Zora Neale Hurston (and later, Chester Himes and James Baldwin) find publishers for their work.

Van Vechten himself published seven novels, all during the Prohibition years; most were semi-autobiographical satires of the cosmopolitan society he loved to skewer. His fascination with black Harlem, however, led him to write a realist novel *Nigger Heaven*—a derogatory slang term used by African Americans at the time to describe the nosebleed seats in the balcony of Harlem night-clubs—which caused a stir when it was first published and divided some in the African-American community.

Zora Neale Hurston, 1938

The black establishment, led by W. E. B. DuBois, was critical of Van Vechten, even though many in their ranks appreciated the spotlight he shined on Harlem's bustling creative community. Most of the book's critics hadn't read the book; they were merely outraged that Van Vechten had used such a title. Others took a different view. In her book-length study *Carl Van Vechten and the Harlem Renaissance*, the African-American literature scholar Emily Bernard puts the controversy into context: "Charles S. Johnson [the famed sociologist] believed the greatest tribute he could offer the book was his regret that a Negro had not written it. Van Vechten's close friend, novelist Nella Larson, shared the sentiment. 'Why, oh why, could we not have done something as big for ourselves?' she lamented to Van Vechten."

"Irony is not anything that most Negroes understand, especially the ones who write for the papers," Van Vechten complained in 1960. Thirty-four years later, he was still disturbed by the negative reaction to the book. "To him," Bernard writes, "the fault lay exclusively with black readers and critics who simply didn't get it." This response underscores Van Vechten's abject narcissism and (at best) inability to have empathy for the African Americans he was writing about.

But why did Van Vechten use the n-word in a book title to begin with? It's not entirely clear. Bernard and White edge closer to finding out, but there's no eureka moment; it seems as if Van Vechten picked the title because he knew it would, if nothing else, cause a lot controversy, and therefore help promote his book. He was right about that.

Bessie Smith, 1936

"THOUGH THE WORLD outside was changing as quickly now as when he first arrived in New York," White writes in the closing pages of his book, "inside the sanctity of his own apartment, Carl Van Vechten was still the only show in town":

> Far more lasting than his output of essays, books, and photography was the example of the life he lived; no other man or woman before him embodied the vision of modern American culture as emphatically ... His twentieth-century urban odyssey made a virtue of racial and sexual diversity and collapsed the nineteenth-century distinctions between edifying art and facile entertainment, constantly probing the boundaries of what was considered good and bad taste.

I agree with much of White's summation. Having read several of the novels, and a selection of his work as a critic, I don't get the sense that you'd want to revisit these works again the way you would, say, those of F. Scott Fitzgerald or even of H. L. Mencken, who were both friendly with Van Vechten. His pre-*Nigger Heaven* fiction is interesting as the precursor to a now more common genre (let's call it "autobiographical hyperbole"), but the writing itself feels dated. (Though I would highly recommend Van Vechten's *The Tiger in the House: A Cultural History of the Cat*, which was brought back into print by the NYRB Classics series in 2007).

More interesting was Van Vechten's status as the dandy hipster of his day, the prototype of the middle-class white kid who goes searching in Harlem for late-night kicks and spiritual nirvana. Norman Mailer would mythologize this character decades later, in his now-infamous 1957 essay "The White Negro."

In his later years Van Vechten found himself a new art form where he could indulge his propensity to archive the present, not to mention his talent for taste-making: photography. And it's his photography—ironically taken up non-professionally, as little more than a hobby—that remains his most striking artistic achievement today.

HAVING DISCOVERED THE portable Leica camera in the early 1930s, Van Vechten took up photography—portraiture, in particular—as a serious art. Over the next thirty years, a coterie of Who's Who would stop by his apartment studio to have their portraits taken, all the while being charmed by the charismatic Carlo. White paints the scene:

> At apartment 7D his shooting space was small and quickly became hot under the studio lights. In coming years he moved to larger premises, but in all his studios there was a closeness, an atmosphere of emotional intimacy. All around lay the clutter of Van Vechten's props and backdrops—crumbled sheets of colored cellophane, posters, rugs, African sculptures, floral wallpaper. To the sitters who arrived this was clearly neither an artist's workroom nor the studio of a commercial artist but the den of an obsessive hobbyist.

Fifty years later, Van Vechten's photography may constitute his most lasting cultural contribution. Although produced in a photo studio, his photographs were never intended for publication (like most professional portraiture of the time), which ended up contributing to their distinct look. Van Vechten's hypnotic charm and the fact that he was able to lower his subject's guard helped him produce some of the most memorable portraits of the artists, writers, actors, singers and performers in his day. Anyone with an internet connection can now go on the Library of Congress website and see thousands of examples for himself. (They're all now deemed public domain, courtesy of Carlo's last will and testament.)

Gertrude Stein, 1935

His portrait of Gertrude Stein, for instance, draped in the American flag, ready to board an ocean liner back to France in the mid-1930s, is the first image I remember seeing of Stein as a high-school student. I had no idea it had been taken by Van Vechten when I first spotted it in a book. But when I examined Van Vechten's portrait of Stein more recently, alongside similarly posed pictures of writer F. Scott Fitzgerald, entertainer Anna May Wong, playwright Eugene O'Neill, actress Lois Moran, artist Georgia O'Keefe, painter Henri Matisse, composer George Gershwin, poet Langston Hughes, singer Bessie Smith and publishers Blanche and Alfred Knopf, some themes and patterns began to appear.

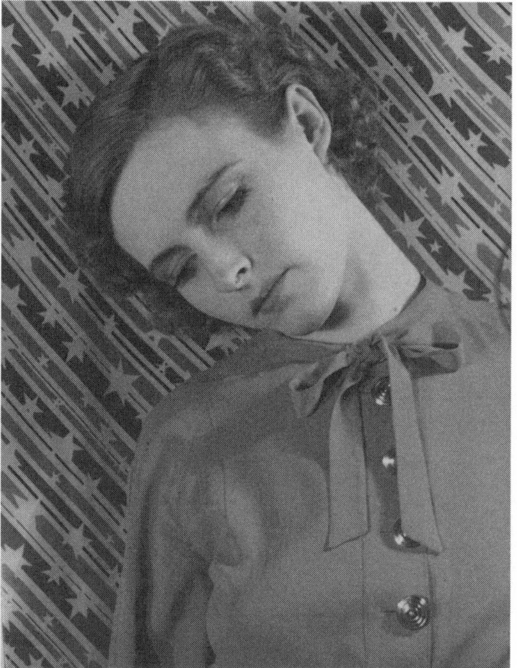

Lois Moran, 1932

Van Vechten was a modernism junkie. But perhaps because he was a writer himself, most of his portraits resemble what has come to be recognized as the quintessential jacket-copy photo for a book: the framed artist brooding into the camera (or looking away, for effect) in a tightly shot style that would be perfect to crop and shrink down for a dust-jacket sleeve layout.

More often than not, the backdrop of the portraits help set the tone for the person being photographed, as if Van Vechten were constructing mini-movie sets for each of his subjects, in stark contrast to the customary white backdrop employed by most of his contemporaries. There is almost a screen-test quality to many of his portraits, and this is both contrived (because of the backdrops and props) and spontaneous (because Van Vechten's cool demeanor and conversationalist personality helped his subjects relax, embrace joviality and give him their best).

One cannot help thinking, while reading through White's biography, that it's too bad Van Vechten didn't start taking pictures sooner. His letters and other correspondence seem ripe with intrigue and a wealth of knowledge for scholars of the Harlem Renaissance, but also for those interested in the period of cultural history between the Jazz Age and the beatnik Fifties. And in photography, Van Vechten found the ideal medium to express himself. One might say that with his photography obsession, he'd found a way to productively channel the insufferable beast within him, the one that craved attention and notoriety, like a child, for everything he did.

Not that Van Vechten's particular brand of narcissism would be considered anything out of the ordinary in today's social-network-obsessed age. And indeed, if you asked people under thirty today who Carl Van Vechten is, most wouldn't have a clue. Although he was a pioneering promoter of the Jazz Age, Van Vechten would be lost in today's postmodern world, trumped by click-bait about an alleged butt implant procedure gone awry. Though, think about this for a second: Van Vechten on the "Allure of Internet Cat Videos" and what it all means. I would buy that for a dollar.

Salvador Dali, 1939

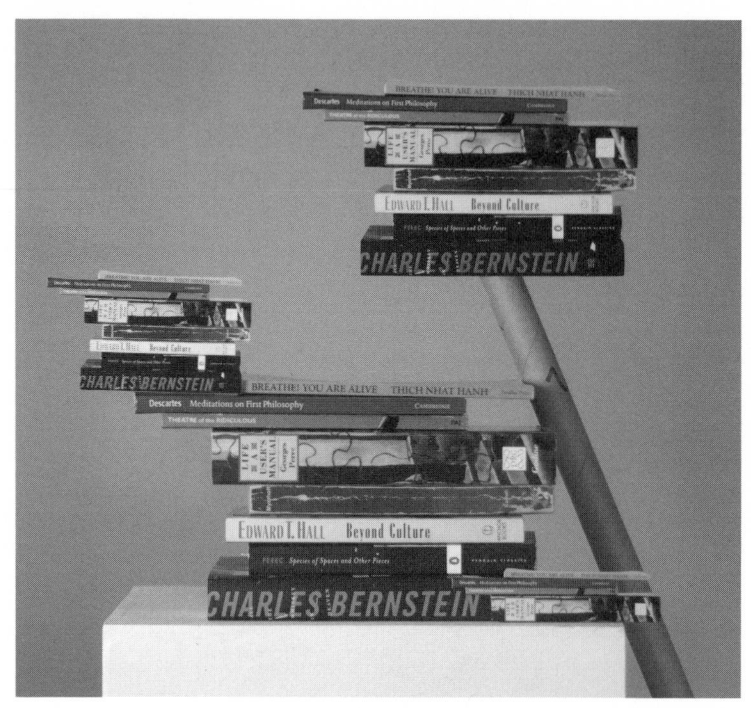

Dane Patterson, *Reread or Returned To (Book Pile)*, 2011

THE IDEA OF A CRITICAL THEORY

by Raymond Geuss

AT THE BEGINNING of the nineteenth century Hegel wrote that every philosopher is a child of his time and none can jump over his own shadow: every philosophy, then, is "its time grasped in a concept." In the twentieth century Adorno took up this idea again when he spoke of the irreducible "kernel of time" embedded in the center of any philosophical view, and of the "temporal index" of truth. Whatever these rather difficult doctrines mean, they clearly are not intended to imply that at any given time all opinions are equally true.

I started a small book in Heidelberg, Germany in 1973 and finally finished it in 1980 at the University of Chicago; *The Idea of a Critical Theory* was published by Cambridge University Press in late 1981. Looking back at the text from the present—from 2013 and my home on this small island off the northwest coast of Europe—I think I can begin to see rather more clearly than I could then some of the relevant features of the historical context within which it was conceived and executed. To return for a moment to Hegel, who is the major spiritual presence hovering over this book—and whose work is the more important for understanding what I was trying to do for not being mentioned at all in the main text—the reader will recall that he also holds that philosophy is essentially retrospective, a reflection of a historical moment or movement that when it finally takes philosophical form is essentially already over. This doctrine marks a distinction between what is "really" happening in the political, social and economic world and the subsequent reflection of this in philosophy (religion, art, law, etc.). As far as what was "really" happening is concerned, we can now see that the period of unprecedented economic growth and political and social progress which took place in the West after the end of World War II began to plateau in the 1970s when productivity began to stagnate. By the early 1970s, though, the assumption that economic growth would continue, levels of prosperity continue to rise, and the social and political structures continue to evolve in the direction of greater flexibility, realism and humanity had become very firmly entrenched in Western populations. The period during which anything like that assumption was at all reasonable was ending just as I was beginning work on my book, although I, of course, did not know that at the time, any more than anyone else did. It would have been political suicide for any major figure in the West to face up to this situation courageously and to try to make clear to the population that the possibilities of relatively easy real growth were exhausted, that the era of ever-increasing prosperity was gone for good; this would have raised intolerable questions about the very foundations of the existing socioeconomic and political order. What the 1980s and 1990s had in store for us, then, was the successive implementation of a series of financial gimmicks which created financial bubbles and allowed the illusion of increasing growth for the majority of the population to be maintained for a while. This cycle was accompanied by a massive change in our culture and socioeconomic system which made possible and in fact actively encouraged individuals and institutions to incur increasingly significant amounts of debt. This, in turn, was attended by a massive shift in resources and economic power away from the majority of the population, a further concentration of wealth in the hands of a very few superlatively rich individuals and families, and a great increase in social inequality. Needless to say, the proliferation of debt *ad libitum* could not continue under existing conditions for long and the system began to collapse in 2007 and 2008. Catastrophe was averted only by a bizarre, not to say perverse, set of political interventions in the Western economies—interventions that have correctly been described as "socialism for the rich": defaulting banks and failing industries were propped up by huge public subsidies, private debts were taken over by the state and profits continued to flow to private investors. This structure, which certainly bears no similarity whatsoever to the ways in which proponents of "capitalism" have described their favored arrangements, seems to give us the worst of all available worlds.

By the end of the 1970s at the very latest, it was visible that a huge countermovement was in progress—it would be incorrect to call it a counterrevolution exactly, since the immediately antecedent period, although one of a certain relative progress, was hardly a revolution. The forms of economic regulation that had been introduced during the Great Depression of the 1930s and had stood the West in good stead for over forty years were gradually relaxed or abolished during the 1980s. Social welfare systems that had gradually been developed came under pressure and began to be dismantled; public services were reduced or "privatized"; infrastructure began to crumble. Inequality, poverty and homelessness grew.

The academic reflection of the massive social and economic changes that took place between 1970 and 1981 could be seen in the gradual marginalization of serious social theory and political philosophy—and of "leftist" thought in particular. The usual story told about the history of "political philosophy" since World War II holds that political philosophy was "dead" until it was revived by John Rawls, whose *Theory of Justice* appeared in 1971. This seems to me seriously misleading. The Forties, Fifties and Sixties, after all, saw the elaboration

of major work by the Frankfurt School (including Marcuse's *One-Dimensional Man*), a rediscovery of Gramsci, various essays and books by Sartre, Camus, de Beauvoir and Merleau-Ponty, Debord's *La Société du Spectacle*, early pieces by Foucault—all works roughly speaking "on the Left." Meanwhile, Popper, Hayek, Leo Strauss and Oakeshott (to name only a few) were active "on the Right." If Anglophones took no notice of this material it was not because serious work in political philosophy failed to exist, but for some other reason. To those engaged (in 1971) in the various and diverse forms of intense political activity which now collectively go under the title of "the Sixties," Rawls's *Theory of Justice* seemed an irrelevance. I completed and defended my doctoral dissertation in the spring of 1971, and I recall my doctoral supervisor, who was a man of the Left but also an established figure and full professor at Columbia University in New York, mentioning to me that there was a new book out by Rawls. In the same breath, he told me that no one would need to read it because it was of merely academic interest—an exercise in trying to mobilize some half-understood fragments of Kant to give a better foundation to American ideology than utilitarianism had been able to provide. Many will think that that was a misjudgment, but I think it was prescient. I cite it in any case to give contemporary readers a sense of the tenor of the 1970s.

Rawls did in fact eventually establish a well-functioning academic industry which was quickly routinized and which preempted much of the space that might have been used for original political thinking. He was one of the forerunners of the great countermovement, proleptically outlining a philosophical version of what came to be known as the "trickle-down" theory. Crudely speaking, this theory eventually takes this form: "Value" is overwhelmingly produced by especially gifted individuals, and the creation of such value benefits society as a whole. Those who are now rich are well-off because they have contributed to the creation of "value" in the past. For the well-off to continue to benefit society, however, they need to be motivated, to be given an incentive. Full egalitarianism will destroy the necessary incentive structure and thus close the taps from which prosperity flows. So inequality can actually be in the interest of the poor because only if the rich are differentially better-off than others will they create value at all—some of which will then "trickle down" or be redistributed to the less well-off. Rawls allows people who observe great inequality in their societies to continue to feel good about themselves, provided that they support some cosmetic forms of redistribution of the crumbs that fall from the tables of the rich and powerful. The apparent gap which many people think exists between the views of Rawls and, say, Ayn Rand is less important than the deep similarity in their basic views. A prison warden may put on a benevolent smile (Rawls) or a grim scowl (Ayn Rand), but that is a mere result of temperament, mood, calculation and the demands of the immediate situation: the fact remains that he is the warden of the prison, and, more importantly, that the prison is a prison. To shift attention from the reality of the prison to the morality, the ideals and the beliefs of the warden is an archetypical instance of an ideological effect. The same holds not just for wardens, but for bankers, politicians, voters, investors, bureaucrats, factory workers, consumers, advisers, social workers, even the unemployed—and, of course, for academics.

In counterpoint to Hegel's view about the philosopher as a child of his time, one might note the views of some other nineteenth-century German thinkers. Nietzsche, for example, took the opposite view. Philosophy is not "its time grasped in concept," he thought, but is by its very nature *unzeitgemäß* ("out of synch with the present time"). The ideal is to be not behind the time but ahead of it, to write a work that would be a philosophy of the future (as Feuerbach tried to do). It is the great hope of many philosophers, particularly political philosophers, to accomplish something like this. If I am right, Rawls did succeed in this aspiration. His project of 1971 came to fruition really only after Reagan, Thatcher and their neoliberal allies had destroyed much of the existing legal, cultural, social, political and economic framework—which patient struggle had built up for several generations in the interests of at least minimally regulating the worst excesses of capitalism.

For these reasons *The Idea of a Critical Theory* was *unzeitgemäß* when it appeared in 1981, espousing views that were about to lose philosophical and political traction in a very serious way. With the current visible collapse of the neoliberal order, though, perhaps it has a chance that was denied it on its original publication. That, of course, does not depend on me.*

---

* *The Idea of a Critical Theory* (1981) has been translated into nine languages. This essay is adapted from the preface to the forthcoming Chinese translation.

SOURCES

THE PROBLEM OF SLAVERY

12 Years a Slave (2013)
David Brion Davis, the Problem of Slavery trilogy
Reinhold Niebuhr, *The Nature and Destiny of Man*

SEARCHING FOR SHANGHAI

André Malraux, *Man's Fate*
W. H. Auden & Christopher Isherwood, *Journey to a War*
Roland Barthes, "Alors, la Chine?"

BUILDING STORIES

Bjarke Ingels, *Yes is More*
David Mazzucchelli, *Asterios Polyp*
Chris Ware, *Building Stories*

MOBILIZING MUTUAL LEARNING

SiS Catalyst, "Children as Change Agents for Science in Society"
Plato, *Republic*

WONDER AND THE ENDS OF INQUIRY

Aristotle, *Metaphysics*
René Descartes, *Passions of the Soul*
Thomas Aquinas, *Summa contra Gentiles*
Francis Bacon, *Novum Organum*
William Wordsworth, "A Poet's Epitaph"

IN PRAISE OF THINGS

John Keats, *Lamia*
W. H. Auden, "Making, Knowing and Judging"
Gerard Manley Hopkins, "As Kingfishers Catch Fire, Dragonflies Draw Flame"

POPULAR SCIENCE

Malcolm Gladwell, *The Tipping Point*
James W. Pennebaker, *The Secret Life of Pronouns*

CHARLIE TROTTER

Charles Bukowski, *Notes of a Dirty Old Man*
History of Political Philosophy, eds. Leo Strauss & Joseph Cropsey

CARL VAN VECHTEN'S PHOTOGRAPHY

Edward White, *The Tastemaker*
Carl Van Vechten, *Nigger Heaven*

THE IDEA OF A CRITICAL THEORY

John Rawls, *A Theory of Justice*
Georg Wilhelm Friedrich Hegel, *Elements of the Philosophy of Right*

CONTRIBUTORS

Adam Alter *is an associate professor of marketing at New York University's Stern School of Business. His most recent book is* Drunk Tank Pink: And Other Unexpected Forces That Shape How We Think, Feel, and Behave *(2013).*

Gordon Arlen *is a Ph.D. student in Political Science at the University of Chicago. He is a former co-editor of* The Art of Theory, *an online journal on the craft of political philosophy.*

D. Graham Burnett *is an editor at* Cabinet *magazine and teaches at Princeton University. He is the author of several books, including* The Sounding of the Whale *(2012).*

Lorraine Daston *is Executive Director of the Max Planck Institute for the History of Science and Visiting Professor in the Committee on Social Thought at the University of Chicago. She has published widely on early-modern knowledge and the history of science, including in* Objectivity *(2010).*

Mark Dion *is a contemporary artist whose sculpture and installation work often engages environmental themes and scientific practices. He teaches in the Visual Arts program at Columbia University.*

Merve Emre *is a doctoral student in English at Yale University. She is an editor at the* Los Angeles Review of Books.

Charles Finch *is a novelist living in Chicago. His most recent novel is* The Last Enchantments *(2014).*

J. C. Gabel *is editor-in-chief of the* Chicagoan *and associate publisher of the* Pitchfork Review.

Raymond Geuss *has recently retired from Cambridge University, where he taught philosophy. The title essay of his most recent book,* A World Without Why, *was published in Issue 2 of* The Point.

Michael D. Gordin *is the Rosengarten Professor of Modern and Contemporary History at Princeton University. His book* Scientific Babel, *a history of the languages of science, will be published by the University of Chicago Press in 2015.*

Lily Huang *is a Ph.D. student in the History of Science at the University of Chicago.*

Jacob Mikanowski *is a writer and critic based in Berkeley. His review of* Mad Men *appeared in Issue 6 of* The Point.

Christian Nakarado *is an architect and designer based in Brooklyn.*

Scott Spillman *is a Ph.D. student in History at Stanford, where he is writing a dissertation on slavery scholarship in America. His essay "Revolutionary History," on the historian Gordon Wood, appeared in Issue 3 of* The Point.

Moira Weigel *is a Ph.D. candidate in the joint program in Comparative Literature and Film and Media at Yale University. She is currently working on a novel about expats in Shanghai.*